HAALAND

MATT AND TOM OLDFIELD

ULTIMATE FOOTBALL HEROES

HAALAND

FROM THE PLAYGROUND
TO THE PITCH

DINO

First published by Dino Books in 2021,
an imprint of Bonnier Books UK,
4th Floor, Victoria House, Bloomsbury Square, London WC1B 4DA
Owned by Bonnier Books,
Sveavägen 56, Stockholm, Sweden

🐦 @UFHbooks
🐦 @footieheroesbks
www.heroesfootball.com
www.bonnierbooks.co.uk

Text © Matt Oldfield 2021
The right of Matt Oldfield to be identified as the author of this work has been
asserted by him in accordance with the Copyright, Designs and Patents Act 1988.

Design by www.envydesign.co.uk

Paperback ISBN: 978 1 78946 475 7
E-book ISBN: 978 1 78946 474 0

British Library cataloguing-in-publication data:
A catalogue record for this book is available from the British Library.

Printed and bound in Great Britain by Clays Ltd, Elcograf S.p.A.

1 3 5 7 9 10 8 6 4 2

For all readers,
young and old(er)

TABLE OF CONTENTS

ACKNOWLEDGEMENTS

First of all, I'd like to thank everyone at Bonnier
Books UK for supporting me throughout and for
running the ever-expanding UFH ship so smoothly.
Writing stories for the next generation of football fans
is both an honour and a pleasure. Thanks also to my
agent, Nick Walters, for helping to keep my dream
job going, year after year.

Next up, an extra big cheer for all the teachers,
booksellers and librarians who have championed these
books, and, of course, for the readers. The success
of this series is truly down to you.

Okay, onto friends and family. I wouldn't be writing
this series if it wasn't for my brother Tom. I owe him

so much and I'm very grateful for his belief in me as an author. I'm also very grateful to the rest of my family, especially Mel, Noah, Nico, and of course Mum and Dad. To my parents, I owe my biggest passions: football and books. They're a real inspiration for everything I do.

Pang, Will, Mills, Doug, Naomi, John, Charlie, Sam, Katy, Ben, Karen, Ana (and anyone else I forgot) – thanks for all the love and laughs, but sorry, no I won't be getting 'a real job' anytime soon!

And finally, I couldn't have done any of this without Iona's encouragement and understanding. Much love to you.

CHAPTER 1

A TROPHY FOR THE TERMINATOR

13 May 2021, Olympiastadion, Berlin

As the Borussia Dortmund team bus slowly weaved through the streets of Berlin towards the stadium, the players fell silent with a mixture of nerves and excitement. The DFB-Pokal cup final was one of the biggest games on the calendar in Germany and there was no doubt about the biggest storyline for this year's final.

Will Erling Haaland win his first major trophy? That had been the number one topic all week, piling on the pressure as Dortmund prepared to face RB Leipzig.

But the man himself was calm. Erling looked out of the window and sipped from his water bottle. He knew that the excitement would kick in once he stepped onto the pitch to warm up; for now, he simply adjusted his headphones and selected a new song on his phone.

Soon, Erling started to see Dortmund fans on the side of the street, waving flags and cheering as they caught sight of the bus. There were lots of 'Haaland 9' shirts, as well as those of his teammates Jadon Sancho and Marco Reus.

Erling was so busy watching the fans that it caught him by surprise when he felt a tap on his shoulder. Erling turned to see Jadon leaning on the seat next to him.

He took off his headphones and gave Jadon a fist bump.

'Ready to put on a show, Terminator?' asked Jadon, grinning.

Erling laughed. That nickname had really stuck, but he actually liked it now. 'Always!' he replied.

In truth, he had felt ready all week. In a season where Dortmund had fallen short of their high goals in the Bundesliga and the Champions League, he was getting sick of the stories about the team's 'potential'. He wanted to respond in the best way he knew – by letting his feet do the talking on the pitch.

'People always seem to talk about us as players for the future,' Erling added. 'This is our chance to remind them that we're already pretty great. We're not just some cute story of a team that could be a contender one day.'

'Yeah, I want to start winning trophies now,' Jadon agreed.

After a quick walk around the pitch, Erling went through his usual pre-game routine. He had done the hard work during the week to get his body into top shape – ice baths, meditation, and even the special glasses to filter the light that his teammates found so funny.

As Erling slotted in his shin pads and taped his ankles, Dortmund manager Edin Terzić clapped his hands and called for quiet in the dressing room.

'Get stuck in from the first whistle,' Edin explained, moving around the room with the same energy that Erling was now feeling. 'We can stretch Leipzig on the counter-attack. When you win the ball back, look directly for Erling and Jadon.'

In the first few minutes, Erling made a quick run to create space. He laid the ball off and then he was on the move again, pulling Leipzig defenders out of position. A pass to the left gave Jadon room to attack, and Erling watched as his teammate curled a beautiful shot past the diving goalkeeper and into the net. 1–0.

'What a start!' Erling shouted, sprinting over to celebrate with his friend.

With Leipzig looking shaky, Erling sensed there would be plenty of opportunities for him. A giveaway in midfield fell to Marco, and immediately Erling knew where the pass would be going. He powered forward and saw Marco's through ball arrowing into his path. Erling had one thought in his mind: make space for a shot. He took one touch to change direction, used his pace to get away from his marker and relied on his strength to brush off a last gasp challenge. Then, in a flash, he shifted his body to poke a low left-footed shot into the bottom corner.

Gooooooooooooooooooooaaaaaaaaaaaaaaaalllllllllllllll llllllllllll!!!!!!!!!!!!!!!!!!!!

'The Terminator strikes again!' Marco yelled as he wrapped Erling in a big hug. 'You're blowing them away.'

By half-time, it was 3–0 and Dortmund were cruising towards the trophy. 'Stay focused!' Edin reminded them in the dressing room when he saw his team looking a bit too relaxed. 'We haven't won anything yet.'

Hungry for more goals, Erling kept closing down Leipzig defenders and making runs through the middle. Leipzig pulled one goal back, but the clock was ticking.

With Leipzig sending more and more players into the box, Erling hovered on the halfway line and knew that he would have a breakaway if his teammates hoofed the ball forward. Sure enough, Dortmund cut out another pass and launched the counter-attack. Suddenly, it was three on one.

Erling raced forward while carefully staying onside. Jadon clipped the ball across to him and Erling had the goal in his sights again. He stumbled slightly as he took the shot, but it still had enough power to fly past the goalkeeper.

Goooooooooooooooooooooaaaaaaaaaaaaaaaaalllllllllllllll llllllllllllll!!!!!!!!!!!!!!!!!!!!

That was the knockout blow. Dortmund were going to be lifting the trophy. Erling jogged over to the corner flag to share the moment with the fans. 'Yeeeeees!' he screamed, raising his arms in the air. Jadon and Marco joined him, as music blared from the stadium's speaker system.

At the final whistle, the Dortmund players tried to soak up every second of such a special moment, and Erling was in the mood to celebrate. With a young squad around him, he hoped this was the first of many major trophies that he would be hoisting in the air.

Erling linked arms with Jadon as the whole squad lined up together and then ran over to where most of the Dortmund fans were still clapping and cheering. It felt good to be sending them off for the summer with these memories.

From a distance, Erling could see the trophy being brought onto the pitch, decorated with black and yellow ribbons. It was almost time! He joined the line and watched his teammates picking from the box of medals. 'Hurry up, guys,' he joked. 'Keep it moving. They're all the same!'

As the party continued back in the dressing room, Erling took a moment to sit down at his locker and admire the medal hanging around his neck. At just twenty years of age, he had big plans for the rest of his career, but the DFB-Pokal cup was a good start. He was on his way to achieving everything he had dreamed about since he was a little boy.

CHAPTER 2

KITTED OUT

On a sunny afternoon, little Erling was sitting on a
bench in the back garden with his brother, Astor.
They had just finished watering the plants with their
matching watering cans when their mother, Gry
Marita, appeared on the path with a tray of milk
and biscuits.

'Daddy's on his way home!' she called, knowing
that her sons had been patiently waiting for him to get
back from training. 'I've told him we'll be out here.'

Soon, she heard footsteps at the gate by the side of
the house.

'Hi, Alfie,' Gry Marita said, waving. She spotted
the bag in his hand. 'Did you get them?' she added,

in a whisper.

Alfie nodded, grinning. 'The sizes aren't quite right but they'll just have to grow into them.'

'I can't wait to see their faces,' Gry Marita replied. 'I've got the camera ready.'

Suddenly, Astor looked over. 'Daddy!' he shouted, and he and Erling scurried across the garden and hugged Alfie's legs.

'Boys, I've got a little surprise for you here,' Alfie said, rustling the bag with excitement in his eyes.

'What is it?' Astor said, trying to grab the bag while Alfie held it just out of reach.

Erling was still too young to fully understand what was happening, but he watched closely and echoed his brother's question: 'What is it?'

'First, have you been good today while I was at training?' Alfie asked.

Both boys smiled their sweetest smiles and nodded. Alfie looked over to Gry Marita for confirmation.

'They really have,' she said. 'They've been sharing toys and enjoying the sunshine. No tantrums, no arguing.'

'Okay then,' Alfie said, looking into the bag to check the sizes. 'I guess I can give you these then.'

As Erling waited patiently, he caught a glimpse of something blue in the bag. Then his dad pulled out a football shirt – no, wait, two football shirts!

'Wow!' Erling and Astor said together as Alfie passed one shirt to each of them.

'Just like Daddy!' Erling said suddenly as he turned the shirt from side to side.

'That's right, son,' Alfie answered. 'This is the Manchester City home shirt that I'll be wearing this season. It seemed about time that you both had one too. What do you think?'

'So cool!' Astor said.

Alfie helped his sons put the shirts over their T-shirts. Sure enough, the shirts almost reached their knees but Erling and Astor didn't care. They were too busy jumping up and down with excitement.

'Thanks, Daddy!' they said, giving Alfie another hug.

Then Astor rushed off with the nearest football. 'Wait for me!' Erling called, following his brother as fast as his little legs would take him.

As Alfie and Gry Marita glanced over, Erling was dribbling the ball towards their little net, taking careful little touches and keeping his balance. 'He loves that ball,' Gry Marita said. 'Though it's probably big enough to knock him over.'

Just when it looked like Astor would tackle his little brother or block his path to the net, he stepped aside and cheered Erling on. 'Go on! Kick it again!'

Finally, Erling reached the goal. He paused, then gave the ball one harder kick. It trickled into the net and Erling raised his arms in the air.

Goooooooooooooooooooaaaaaaaaaaaaaaaaalllllllllllllll llllllllllll!!!!!!!!!!!!!!!!!!!

'A natural goalscorer!' Alfie said quietly, turning to Gry Marita.

She rolled her eyes. 'I should have known you'd be trying to sign him up already.'

'Do you want to try it again?' they heard Astor ask. To their surprise, Erling nodded and scooped the ball out of the net.

With his new Manchester City shirt flapping in the wind, Erling ran and ran until he eventually lay down on the grass.

When it became clear that this was the end of the afternoon football, Alfie walked over and crouched down next to Erling. His son's cheeks were red and his hair was sweaty, but he was still grinning.

'Come on, sharpshooter,' Alfie said. 'Time for your bath.'

CHAPTER 3

LEAVING ENGLAND

Once Alfie had made the decision to retire from football, it sparked other important conversations in the Haaland house. They had moved to England – first Nottingham, then Leeds, then Manchester – for his football career and the chance to play in the Premier League. But beyond that, their plans had always been open.

'Now feels like the right time to move home to be closer to friends and family,' Gry Marita said. 'I know it'll be a change for us all, but we can make it work. What do you think?'

'Well, the longer we wait, the more difficult it will be to take the kids away from their school and their friends here. I think you're right that this is our chance to give them a Norwegian childhood. It's just such a big decision.'

Gry Marita nodded and neither of them spoke for a few minutes as they thought about all the work involved in moving countries.

Alfie sighed. 'We're going to need a lot of boxes!' he said, and they both burst out laughing.

Once they had decided to move back to Norway, the next question was which city they would pick. That proved to be an easier discussion, with both parents confident that Bryne, a small town where Alfie had played early in his career, was the right choice to raise their young family. Now they just had to tell the kids.

After dinner one night, Alfie piled the dirty plates next to the sink and sat down next to Gry Marita. 'Kids, we want to talk to you about something,' he said. 'Now that I'm not playing football in England anymore, we've decided it's time for a new adventure – one that brings you closer to your family and your roots. These years in England have been amazing and we wouldn't swap them for anything. But it's time to go home to Norway.'

Alfie paused and looked around the table at his three children. Erling was still too small to voice an opinion but the two older Haaland kids, Gabrielle and Astor, understood. The questions came in waves.

'When are we leaving? Where will we live? Can I bring all my toys? Will we ever come back to England?'

As Alfie and Gry Marita gave them the answers to each individual question, they could see their children's concern and confusion turning to excitement.

'You're going to love it!' Alfie said. 'Bryne is a great town for kids – lots of parks, lots of playgrounds. I was there for a few years when I was just getting started as a footballer, and the people are so nice.'

'You'll also get to meet Albert, your new little cousin,' Gry Marita added.

Before long, this new adventure was the only thing that Astor and Gabrielle wanted to talk about. Even Erling was proudly listing all the toys and games that he wanted to pack.

Finally, moving day arrived, and Erling stood on a

chair at the window to watch all their things being loaded onto a big truck. 'Don't worry,' Gabrielle said. 'It'll all be there in Norway when we get there.'

Still, it was a strange feeling for Erling. For weeks, he had seen the packing boxes around the house, but it didn't seem real – until now. Alfie brought him for one last look at his old bedroom and then they waved goodbye to the house as they drove off down the street.

The flight to Norway provided more excitement. On the plane, Erling, Astor and Gabrielle scooped their backpacks onto their laps and started looking inside to see what their parents had packed for them.

As they pulled out each item, they shrieked with excitement. 'Cool!' Erling said, holding up a new magazine. He also found two of his favourite books, his prized teddy bear and a bag of snacks.

'Norway, here we come!' Astor said, as the plane moved down the runway ready for take-off.

For the next few months, Erling felt like he was camping indoors, with clothes everywhere and bedroom furniture arriving piece by piece. As the

Haalands slowly unpacked the endless pile of boxes, their new house in Bryne began to feel like home.

Soon, Erling's new bedroom started to take shape too. As he lay on his bed and looked up at the tiny sliver of light peeking through the curtains, he smiled. He had a good feeling about Bryne and the life that he would have there.

CHAPTER 4

BRYNE BEGINNINGS

'We need to leave in ten minutes,' Alfie called on his way up the stairs. 'We can't be late for your first football practice.'

Erling shoved the last morsel of his sandwich into his mouth and picked up his water bottle from the table. His backpack was already at the front door with his boots and a fresh T-shirt. He slipped the bottle into a side pocket.

He had been looking forward to this practice for weeks – he must have checked the date hundreds of times since his parents told him that he would be playing for a real team. Not just any team either – the same team that his dad had played for many years earlier.

'I'm ready!' he shouted.

'You'll need these too,' Alfie replied, passing Erling a brand new pair of shin pads. 'We've got to protect your legs while you're dribbling past everyone.'

Erling's eyes lit up. He was going to look like a real footballer now.

The traffic was faster than expected so they arrived fifteen minutes early, but Erling was glad to have some time to look around. He looped his backpack over one shoulder and followed Alfie over to the main building.

As they opened the door, they almost bumped into a man in a Bryne tracksuit.

'Great to see you, Alfie!' the man said, grinning. He turned to Erling. 'Welcome to Bryne, young man. I'm Alf Ingve Berntsen, but you can call me Coach Berntsen. I work with all the age groups here.'

Erling shook hands with him and gave a shy smile.

'Don't worry,' Coach Berntsen said. 'We'll get you on the pitch in no time, but let's have a quick chat while we wait for the other kids to get here.'

But Erling's eyes had already been drawn to the sign across from the reception desk, pointing the way to the indoor gym. 'Can I see the indoor pitch first?' he asked.

Coach Berntsen nodded. 'Of course. Follow me.'

He led the way down a wide corridor, past the changing rooms, and stopped outside double doors with glass windows. Inside, Erling could see two nets, a pile of footballs and a stack of cones. A man and a woman, both wearing the same sweatshirt as Coach Berntsen, were busy arranging cones in the far corner of the gym.

'We're just getting things set up for tonight,' Coach Berntsen explained. 'It's not the newest or flashiest academy in the country, but we're really proud of what we've created here. We've got a group of forty kids at most age groups, with a mix of boys and girls.'

Erling was half-listening while still staring through the window.

'You may as well drop off your coat and get your boots on now,' Coach Berntsen said, pointing back the way they had walked. 'Your dad can take you to the changing room while I get the academy forms ready.'

Once he had his boots and shin pads on, Erling

headed back towards the gym. By now, other boys and girls were arriving and a little crowd had gathered at the gym door, waiting to be let inside.

'Just enjoy it,' Alfie said, putting his arm around Erling's shoulders. 'This is about having fun.'

Once the kids were inside, the scene was just like what Erling was used to at the park. Bags were thrown in one corner and they all took turns taking shots at one of the goals. One of the boys passed the ball to Erling. He took a touch and could feel all the eyes watching him. He hit a good shot that clipped the crossbar.

'Listen up, everyone,' Coach Berntsen said, blowing his whistle and prompting everyone to huddle around him. 'We've got a new face with us today. Give a big Bryne welcome to Erling.' He pointed across the circle and Erling waved. All the boys and girls waved back and smiled.

They started off with a few laps around the gym. Straightaway, Erling felt like a real footballer as Coach Berntsen shouted out instructions like 'Up' to jump for a pretend header and 'Down' to touch one hand to the floor. Once all the boys and girls had worked up a bit of a sweat, Coach Berntsen moved on to some passing drills. Erling was paired up with a boy called Christian and they were soon guiding the ball back and forth across the width of the gym.

For the last fifteen minutes of the session, Coach Berntsen set up some mini pitches and split the kids into eight teams. Erling was on the blue team with two boys and a girl, who all seemed to know each other well.

'Ready to crush the red team, Erling?' one of the boys asked.

Erling laughed. 'Of course!' he replied.

'Good! I'm Stig, this is John and this is Sara,' he said, pointing to the others.

They all bumped fists.

'We've got to win this week,' Stig said. 'We lost 4–0 last week and…'

But there was no time for Stig to finish his sentence. Coach Berntsen blew his whistle and threw a ball onto the pitch. Game on!

'I'll drop back with Sara, and you go forward with John,' Stig called out as he turned to chase one of the red-team players.

The blue-team quickly got the ball back as Sara cleared it to Stig, who dribbled forward and looked up. Erling sprinted behind the last red-team defender. 'Pass it through!' he called, waving his arm to get Stig's attention.

Stig poked the ball forward and Erling got to it first. Two red shirts rushed towards him, but Erling knew what he wanted to do. At the last second, instead of rushing a quick shot, he spun and flicked the ball with the outside of his foot so that it rolled slowly across to John for a simple tap-in. *GOAL!*

'How did you know I'd be there?' John asked, amazed by the perfect pass.

Erling shrugged with a big grin all over his face. 'They were all running over to me. I just sensed you'd be open.'

That got Coach Berntsen's attention too. 'Nice pass, Erling!' he shouted, clapping. Coach Berntsen usually tried to keep an eye on all four of the mini games, but how could he leave now after that little piece of magic?

After a near-miss from the red team, Stig scuffed a goal kick towards John and ran forward for a return pass. John had other ideas and turned inside instead, trying to make space for a shot. A blue-team defender darted forward to tackle him, but the ball bounced loose to Erling. Without even thinking, Erling poked the ball through to where he had seen Stig making the earlier run. Stig had all the time in the world to cushion the pass and make it 2–0. *GOAL!*

Stig ran over for a high-five. 'That was amazing, Erling. Even I couldn't miss that one!'

By now Coach Berntsen had called over to one of the other coaches and was busy recapping how Erling's two perfect touches had led to goals.

There was still time for Erling to score one himself too. With the whole red team stuck at the other end of the pitch, Sara intercepted a pass and set Erling through on goal. He took one touch with his left foot, then rolled the ball carefully into the net with his right foot.

Gooooooooooooooooooooaaaaaaaaaaaaaaaallllllllllllll llllllllllll!!!!!!!!!!!!!!!!!!!

Up in the small viewing area, Alfie smiled a proud smile. His son certainly knew how to make a big impression.

CHAPTER 5

RECORD-BREAKER

Alfie and Gry Marita quickly found that football wasn't the only sport where Erling had star talent. He was a natural at handball and was starting to get a taste for athletics too.

As Gry Marita waited in the school car park, she spotted Erling in the middle of the playground talking to one of the teachers. It looked like a serious conversation, and the teacher seemed to be writing something on a clipboard. 'Uh-oh,' she mumbled under her breath.

When Erling walked slowly to the car, he had a small slip of paper in his hand. He opened the door and climbed into his seat. Gry Marita waited patiently for her son to explain. After a few minutes of silence, she gave up.

'Are you going to tell me why that teacher stopped you?' she asked, looking at Erling in the car mirror.

Erling's cheeks went red. 'You saw that?'

'Yes,' Gry Marita replied. 'Did you get in trouble?'

Erling shook his head. 'No, nothing like that. That teacher is the one who runs most of the sports sessions. We did long jump today and he said I did really well.'

Gry Marita smiled. That was certainly better than some of the scenarios she was imagining. 'Was that whole conversation about long jump then?'

'Yes, he thinks I should sign up for the Under-6 athletics events.' Erling waved the slip of paper. 'There's a competition this weekend.'

Back at home, Alfie and Gry Marita checked the details and completed the registration.

'No pressure,' Alfie explained. 'Just try your best.'

On Saturday morning, Erling woke up even earlier than usual. He prepared a bowl of cereal as quietly as he could and then checked that his trainers were by the front door.

On the way to the local athletics club, Gry Marita played some of Erling's favourite songs to help him relax. But he mainly looked excited. If there was one thing she knew about her son, it was that he loved to compete. He had that usual sparkle in his eyes.

They checked in at the first booth and Erling was given a number to clip onto his shorts. Gry Marita joined the other parents by the edge of the track and found the spot with the best view of the long jump sandpit.

Erling sat quietly as more and more boys and girls arrived at the athletics club, with some of them joining him for the long jump. A man in a yellow shirt appeared next to the sandpit, ready to measure each jump based on where the jumper's feet landed.

Finally, his name was called and Erling managed a few final stretches before lining up in the starting position. 'Good luck!' Gry Marita called.

Erling took a deep breath and looked at the sandpit in front of him. Making sure that he was behind the white line, he bent his knees and launched himself into the sandpit. Sand flew up on both sides.

'That's a fair jump,' one of the judges called out. The second judge was huddled around the mark in the sand.

'It's not just a fair jump,' the second judge replied. 'It's also a huge jump! That's got to be a record for a five-year-old.'

Erling waited patiently to make sure that he understood what had just happened.

'How far was my jump?' he asked.

'163 centimetres,' came the answer. 'That's... that's... well, I've never seen anything like that.'

As Erling jogged back to join the rest of the boys, he tried not to show his excitement. He didn't want them to feel bad. Standing as close to the long jump sandpit as he could, Erling watched the next three boys take their turns. One overstepped the jump line, and the other two were well short of Erling's mark.

It was soon clear that Erling was going to win. As the judges congratulated him, he saw his mum walking over with another judge who he had seen earlier at the main booth.

'We've checked our record books, Erling, and you'll be the latest addition,' the judge said with a big smile. 'Your jump today is a new national record for the Under-6 category.'

Erling didn't know what to say. He just looked at his mum, first in shock and then with a wide smile.

That night, as Alfie put five plates on the table and the family sat down for dinner, the phone rang. Gry Marita answered, and Erling could faintly hear his mum's side of the conversation.

'Oh hello, yes, of course I remember. How did the rest of the event go?'

Then: 'Really? In the whole world? Wow, that's unbelievable. I'm with him now and I'll let him know. He's going to be stunned.'

As Gry Marita picked up a glass of water and sat down at the table, the rest of family fell silent. 'So, what was that about?' Alfie asked.

'Well, it turns out that our little Erling set a pretty big new record today,' she said.

Erling was confused. 'But, Mum, we already knew that. That judge told us.'

Gry Marita smiled. 'Yes, this afternoon he told us it was a record in Norway.' She paused. 'Tonight he wanted us to know that it was actually the longest recorded jump by a five-year-old... in the world!'

Erling just stared with his mouth wide open. 'What?!' he finally managed to reply. He glanced at Astor and Gabrielle, who both looked shocked too.

'Markus, the main judge, said he was sure he'd never heard of a jump like that in any of the kids' events he'd done and he checked with some of the other judges he knows in other countries. They found an archive with all the details and... 1.63 metres is a new world record for this age group.'

'My brother, the world beater!' Astor said, proudly reaching over and raising Erling's arm into the air to show he was a champion.

Once all three children were in bed, Gry Marita joined Alfie on the sofa. 'Erling is certainly full of surprises,' she said, yawning. 'What a day!'

Alfie grinned. 'Something tells me that this is just the first of many times that we'll be celebrating one of Erling's big achievements,' he replied.

CHAPTER 6

STRIKER'S INSTINCTS

When Erling had first joined Bryne, he remembered Coach Berntsen, Stig and some of the other kids asking him what position he played. Back then, he had just shrugged. Usually, he was wherever the ball was. If that meant running back to be a defender, that was what he did.

But after six months in the Bryne academy, Erling now knew his answer. 'I'm a striker,' he would tell any of the new academy arrivals when he introduced himself.

Alfie was quick to remind his son that there was no need to make any decisions on that just yet. 'I played a few different positions when I was your age. It was only later that I decided to be more of a defender. Even then, I sometimes played in midfield too.'

Deep down, though, Alfie knew that Erling would always be a striker. He could already see the similarities between his son and some of the great strikers he had played with during his career – the joy of scoring goals, the ruthlessness to keep looking for chances even after he had scored a few and the disappointment all over his face in any game where he didn't find the back of the net.

Plus, he always wanted to learn. One morning, when most boys his age were probably watching cartoons or playing outside, Erling was more interested in knowing more about the star strikers that his dad had played alongside over the years.

'Well, I played with different types of strikers,' Alfie said, quickly thinking through his time at Nottingham Forest, Leeds and Manchester City. 'Jimmy Floyd Hasselbaink was incredible at Leeds. With him, it was the power of his shot that always gave him an edge. Robbie Fowler had incredible instincts and just always seemed to be in the right place at the right time. With

Nicolas Anelka, it was all about his pace.'

Erling nodded and, not for the first time, thought how impressive it was that his dad had played at that level. 'Okay, so I guess there's no set formula for becoming a great striker then,' he said.

'That's right. There's no "right way" to do it. But when I think about those strikers I saw every day in training, there was one thing they all had in common: cool, calm, ruthless finishing. They all lived for those goalscoring chances.'

Erling was determined to show that he lived for those moments too. As he helped to pick up the cones at the end of one practice, sweat trickled down his face. He brushed it off with his hand. Just then, Coach Berntsen walked over with Alfie.

'Great practice again today, Erling,' Coach Berntsen said. 'That goal at the end was unstoppable.'

Erling smiled.

'Listen,' Coach Berntsen continued, 'I've been talking to your dad because we think you're ready for some tougher tests. Next month, we'd like to move you up to the Under-12s group. How does that sound?'

Erling hesitated. He had made some good friends in the Under-6 team. But how could he turn down the chance to challenge himself against better players? If Coach Berntsen thought he was ready, that was good enough for Erling.

'Great!' Erling said, trying to shake off the doubts. 'That'll push me to keep getting better because I'm sure those kids won't go easy on me.'

'Exactly,' Coach Berntsen said. 'We want you to be comfortable being uncomfortable on the football pitch, if that makes any sense, so we'll keep throwing you into these situations. You'll be learning on the fly but you're good enough to soak it all in.'

Erling was still in a daze as he showered and changed. He really needed to sit down for a few minutes to digest this news.

'This is really exciting,' Alfie explained in the car on the way home, sensing that his son was deep in thought. 'Coach Berntsen told me that he doesn't suggest this kind of thing very often, but he sees the special talent you have. Remember, there's no pressure. Just give it a try. If you're not enjoying it in the Under 12s, we can have another conversation with Coach Berntsen.'

Erling nodded. 'Thanks, Dad! At training, sometimes I hear the way other parents are shouting at their kids and it's like they want the kids to become professionals more than the kids themselves want it. I'm so glad that you're not like that.'

'We just want you to be happy,' Alfie replied. 'If that means rising through the different age groups at Bryne and becoming a professional, that's great. But you have to do what's right for you. Just because I was a footballer doesn't mean that you have to follow in my footsteps. We'll support your decisions no matter what.'

Erling smiled, then went back to looking out of the window. He felt better. He had moved on from the fears and was already picturing the goals he would score in the Under-12 sessions. Big possibilities lay ahead – and he knew it.

CHAPTER 7

CATCHING
THE EYE

Erling continued to grow – in height, in confidence and in skill level. As the Bryne Under 14s changed into their boots and began to warm up, Erling ran over to the nearest ball. He flicked it into the air, controlled it on his thigh and volleyed it into the empty net. He spotted another ball and went through the same routine – flick, thigh, volley. The shot arrowed into the top corner.

'Don't you ever get tired of scoring?' his teammate Patrick said, laughing as he jogged past.

'I think you already know the answer to that!' Erling fired back, grinning.

While most of the other boys were stretching or

gently running from touchline to touchline, Erling preferred to be shooting to get his body warm. Sure, he would join in for a little running and stretching before kick-off, but nothing helped him focus as much as feeling the ball ping off his foot and into the net.

Coach Berntsen called the boys over for a final huddle. 'Move the ball,' he said, gesturing with his hands from side to side. 'Remember the last time we played this team? We tried too many solo runs instead of patiently passing our way through. Keep that in mind.'

Erling certainly hadn't forgotten that game. It was such a frustrating afternoon. He had been tightly marked the whole time, sometimes by two defenders, and he had wasted some good chances by rushing shots instead of setting up his teammates. 'Today will be different,' he said under his breath as the referee blew his whistle.

Part of his plan was to make runs out to the wings. Last time, he had mostly stayed in a central position, making it easier for the defenders to stick close to him. As Bryne broke forward, he peeled away to the right

and saw that his marker hadn't tracked him there.
'Square it!' he called, positioning himself to hit a first-
time shot. The pass was hit hard but Erling knew that
taking a touch to control it would allow the defenders
to recover. So he thumped a quick strike with his left
foot and watched in delight as it flew into the roof of
the net.

*Goooooooooooooooooooaaaaaaaaaaaaaaaaalllllllllllllll
lllllllllllll!!!!!!!!!!!!!!!!!!!!!*

'Get in!!!!' he shouted. Patrick was fired up too,
racing over to give Erling a double high-five.

Another quick breakaway brought the same result.
This time, Erling let the ball roll over to his right foot
and then fired a shot past the goalkeeper's dive.

*Goooooooooooooooooooaaaaaaaaaaaaaaaaalllllllllllllll
lllllllllllll!!!!!!!!!!!!!!!!!!!!!*

By now, his teammates had come to expect this
type of performance from Erling. They looked to
him so often that Coach Berntsen would repeatedly
remind the other boys to have more confidence in
themselves to go on a dribbling run or take a shot.

A week later, Erling kept up his goalscoring form.

Whenever he lined up a shot on his left foot, there was a buzz of excitement on the touchline – and for a good reason. Against another of Bryne's rivals, Erling's corner was blocked and the ball cannoned back to him. He took a touch to beat the first defender, then rocketed a shot past the goalkeeper at the near post from an almost impossible angle.

Goooooooooooooooooooaaaaaaaaaaaaaaaallllllllllllll llllllllllll!!!!!!!!!!!!!!!!!!

Erling was willing to take that kind of shot from any angle, whether he had dribbled out towards the touchline or was standing over a free kick just inside the halfway line. The opposition usually knew what was coming – sometimes he would even see players reluctant to get into the wall against his free kicks – but often they could do nothing to stop it.

As Erling sped behind the defence and sealed another Bryne win with an unstoppable shot, there were cheers and shouts from the parents and coaches on the touchline. He looked over to where Alfie was standing and beamed when he saw his dad nodding his head and clapping.

At the final whistle, Alfie walked over to bring Erling his water bottle. 'That was outstanding, son. Two great goals. Keep working hard – all that effort is paying off.'

In the car on the way home, Erling looked over at Alfie. He had a question that he wanted to ask, but he was trying to find the right words. Eventually, he plucked up the courage.

'Dad, what else do you see when you watch my games? I know you'll probably say I'm only thirteen and just scoring goals should be good enough for me, but I really value your opinion.'

Alfie glanced over at Erling. 'You're only thirteen and just scoring goals should be good enough for you,' he said, smiling.

Erling laughed. 'Come on! Tell me!'

'Well, I can give you a few suggestions. First, keep working on your heading. With the way you can jump, you'll win headers against almost anyone, but directing them on target is an important skill to master. That will make you a more complete striker.'

Erling nodded and screwed up his face as he

remembered a header he had missed in the game. 'That's a good one.'

'The other thing is more complicated: what it means to be a team's star player. As you know, I played with some great players and, as someone who was usually part of the supporting cast, I can tell you how important it was for the star players to not only lead by example but also make the players around them better too.'

Erling listened carefully, but he wasn't sure if he fully understood. 'So, should I be passing the ball more or... is...?'

'Not necessarily. Your teammates count on you to hit those spectacular shots and take risks with the ball. But, in the years ahead... and yes, I mean *in the years ahead*, part of your role will be to build up their confidence and help them shine in their roles. Sometimes that means words of encouragement; other times that means getting on their case. With every youth level you go through, the value of playing as a team increases.'

'I get it,' Erling said. 'That's great advice. Have you

considered getting into coaching? I'd be happy to give you a good reference!'

They both laughed as Alfie parked in the driveway. 'Well, son, that's the least you can do after all my years cleaning your boots!' he said.

CHAPTER 8

ZLATAN

As Alfie sleepily flipped through different TV channels one morning, Erling was curled up on the sofa next to him. He would need to start getting ready for school soon, but he decided he could spare a few more minutes.

Suddenly, something caught Erling's eye on the TV. 'Dad, go back!' he said excitedly. In the quiet room, it came out louder than he had intended. Startled for a second, Alfie looked around for the TV remote. Finding it under a cushion, he pressed the BACK button and a football round-up show appeared on the screen.

Gry Marita put her head round the door. 'Erling, come on!' she said. 'Time to get moving.'

'He's just watching these highlights and then I'll

send him up,' Alfie replied, with a small grin. 'It was Erling's idea, I promise.'

Gry Marita smiled and shook her head. 'Oh, and I'm sure you took a lot of convincing to put the football on!'

Erling had barely noticed their conversation. He was glued to the action. First, Cristiano Ronaldo was tormenting two helpless defenders. Erling found himself leaning forward on the sofa every time Ronaldo set off on a dribbling run. He had his hands over his face as Ronaldo fired an unsaveable shot into the top corner. 'Did you see that?' he asked Alfie, standing up and moving even closer to the TV. 'What a goal!'

Then, it was Zlatan Ibrahimović, flicking the ball with the heel of his boot and volleying the ball against the post. Erling had already started 'being Zlatan' whenever he and his friends decided to play as a pretend dream team in the park, but this was another chance to see his hero in action.

Seconds later, there was another Zlatan clip from the same game. This time, he controlled the ball effortlessly on his chest, let it drop to his right foot and then flicked it over the head of the defender rushing towards him. It was tricks like this that Erling would watch once and remember forever.

'Imagine if you could combine Zlatan and Ronaldo into one player!' he said to Alfie. 'The strength, the tricks, the vision and the goals.' He paused for a moment to picture what that player would look like.

'Erling, that player you're describing could be you one day,' Alfie said.

Erling laughed and turned around, expecting his dad to be grinning at that joke. But there was no smile.

'I'm serious,' Alfie said. 'You can do it all. You're tall like Zlatan and you're getting stronger. Plus, your footwork is way better than you think it is.'

'Well, as my dad, you're a little biased, I think,' Erling said, laughing. 'But, if we're dreaming big, one day I'd love for the Norway fans to feel the same way about me as the Sweden fans feel about Zlatan! That must be an incredible feeling.'

Maybe it was the fact that Sweden was so close to Norway, but Erling felt a connection to Zlatan – even the off-field Zlatan, who liked to make bold comments and give reporters a hard time. He never gave boring answers and Erling admired the way that he always seemed to back up his words on the pitch.

While some of Erling's friends gave him a strange look when he automatically said 'Zlatan' whenever he was asked about his football idol, there was no-one else who played the game quite like him.

That evening, as he and Astor kicked a ball back and forth in the garden, Erling tried to copy some of those Zlatan moves. He could manage the chest control but the instant flick over Astor ended with Erling slipping backwards onto the grass.

'That one isn't as easy as Zlatan makes it look!' Erling said, as his brother helped him up. 'I think I'll need to see that clip again.'

'Well, I could easily see Zlatan playing until he's forty,' Astor said. 'So if you hurry up and get a big move, you might still have a chance to play against him!'

CHAPTER 9

HALFWAY LINE
HERO

The more games that Erling played, the more he dreamed of one day playing for the senior Norway team. 'Keep working hard and the opportunities will come,' Alfie assured him.

There was lots of encouragement along the way too. A call-up to the Norway Under-15 squad to play Sweden felt like a positive step forward and Erling was full of confidence as he arrived at the team hotel. He felt good in the two short practices, especially the shooting drills where he hit the target consistently with either foot. It was like he was back in the gym in Bryne, taking layoffs from Coach Berntsen. A couple of times he saw the goalkeeper wiggling his fingers because of the power of one of Erling's shots.

Practices were fun, but Erling lived for the games. As he went through the warm up, he occasionally glanced over at the clock on the far side of the pitch, beyond where the Sweden players were stretching, to check how many minutes before the real action started.

Finally, it was time. Erling jumped on the spot and stretched his neck from side to side as he waited for the referee to walk over to the centre circle for the kick-off. He knew the nervous feeling in his stomach would disappear as soon as the whistle blew.

As the referee hurried over, Erling looked up and spotted the Sweden goalkeeper and one of their defenders talking just outside the penalty area. Why wasn't he in his goal? When Norway took the kick-off, the ball was laid back to Erling and he saw the conversation had just finished at the edge of the box. The Sweden goal was still wide open.

As he controlled the ball, Erling heard his teammates calling for a short pass, but he had other ideas. He swung his foot back and then launched a long, looping shot towards the Sweden goal. By now, the goalkeeper

had spotted the danger and was rushing back towards
his line. But he was a step too late. Despite his
desperate dive, the ball bounced just before the line
and dropped into the net.

*Gooooooooooooooooooooaaaaaaaaaaaaaaaaallllllllllllllll
llllllllll!!!!!!!!!!!!!!!!!!!!!!*

For a few seconds, there was a stunned silence
around the pitch as everyone took in what had just
happened. Erling stood with his arms in the air as his
teammates jumped on his back. Like most of the boys,
he was still in shock himself.

At half-time, one of the Norway coaches came over
to give Erling a high-five. 'Hardly anyone would have
seen the chance to shoot there, even fewer would have
tried the shot, and even fewer would have got it on
target,' he said. 'Just incredible.'

For the rest of the game, Erling felt like he was
walking on air. He just kept thinking about that
moment when the ball dropped softly into the net.
He could be in that position again a hundred times and
never come close to hitting the shot as perfectly.

Erling could also sense that the Sweden defenders

were still angry about being embarrassed by his goal, especially with all the screams and shouts from the Norway substitutes. In the second half, he felt an arm in his back every time the ball was played forward to him, but he kept his cool.

'Going to have a few bruises tomorrow?' another of the Norway coaches asked back in the dressing room after the game.

Erling just smiled. 'Nothing I can't handle,' he said, looking down at the cuts on his knee and shin. 'I think that referee just had a different definition of a foul.'

As Erling walked out to the team bus with a little limp, Kasper, one of the team's defenders, appeared next to him. 'So, come on, put us out of our misery,' he said.

Erling looked at him, confused. 'What do you mean?'

Kasper grinned. 'Tell us how many weeks we're going to be hearing about that goal for.'

Now it was Erling's turn to grin. 'Weeks? I think you mean months! Just be thankful that no-one got it on video!'

As he sat down in an empty row near the front of

the bus, he leaned back against the headrest and closed his eyes. 'How could anyone not love football?' he whispered to himself.

CHAPTER 10

A BOY
AMONG MEN

Back in Erling's earliest days at Bryne, Coach Berntsen had made it very clear that he would continue to challenge him by moving him to older age groups whenever he seemed ready. He had always been true to his word.

That latest step meant joining the Bryne reserves and sharing the pitch with grown men for the first time. For a skinny fifteen-year-old who was still learning the game, this represented a big change, and Erling knew it.

Alfie and Gry Marita had mixed feelings about it. On the one hand, this was another sign that Erling was on the path to becoming a professional footballer and they knew how much this journey meant to him. But equally the idea of their young son being thrown around by thirty-year-olds in a physical reserves league was hardly comforting.

But they all agreed it was only fair to give it a shot and see how it went. That way, there could be no regrets.

The two things that Erling had in his favour were pace and quick feet – and those strengths made a difference, both in scoring goals and avoiding injuries. He was also fearless and that quickly won over his teammates as he slid in for tackles and went in for headers against players who often weighed twice as much as he did. In turn, his teammates protected him, taking issue with any opponents who tried to intimidate him.

With eighteen goals in fourteen games, Erling usually had the last laugh – and the experience also reminded him that, however scrappy a goal, they still all counted. One wet Saturday afternoon, nothing was going right for Erling. He was overhitting passes, struggling to control the ball and rushing the few chances that came his way. He slapped his thigh in frustration as his heavy touch slowed down the latest promising counter-attack.

As the ball rolled out for a throw-in, Erling saw Alfie walking up the touchline, closer to the action. The throw-in went down the line and was booted out of play again, even further this time. With a quick wiggle of his finger, Alfie called Erling over. 'I know it hasn't been your day so far, but keep getting into the box. With weather like this, you'll get another chance.'

That gave Erling an extra boost of energy. He stopped drifting out wide as often and made sure that he was always alert when crosses or shots came in. Then Tord, another youngster, fizzed a low shot through a crowded penalty area. It skipped off the wet surface and the goalkeeper just about palmed the ball out. But now it was loose in the six-yard box. Erling had already turned to follow the path of the shot and was a crucial step ahead of the three nearest defenders. He slid, gathering momentum as water splashed up from the pitch, and stabbed the ball over the line.

Goooooooooooooooooooooaaaaaaaaaaaaaaaaalllllllllllllll lllllllllllll!!!!!!!!!!!!!!!!!!!!!

It was probably the ugliest goal that Erling had ever scored in a game, but his teammates reacted like it was a thirty-yard screamer. They wrapped him in hugs and then all fell on the ground. Erling didn't care. He was already soaked from the rain and filthy from his sliding goal. Plus, now Bryne were winning.

As he jogged back to the halfway line, he looked over at Alfie on the touchline and his dad grinned back, waving his finger in the air. Erling rolled his eyes and got ready for an 'I told you so!' on the drive home.

The rain continued to pour down, but Erling had a second burst of energy after his goal. He tracked back to help the midfield again and again, and he slid in for two important blocks as Bryne clung onto their lead. At the final whistle, he pumped his fists and crouched down to catch his breath. He was going to be sore in the morning, but they had won. That's what mattered.

Even after a hot shower, Erling was still shivering as he threw on a hoodie and tracksuit bottoms. Every single player stopped to shake his hand on the way out of the dressing room and gave him more praise for this scrappy, scrambled winner than when he had scored two amazing solo goals in the last game.

Erling smiled as he flung his water bottle and shin pads into his kitbag. He had clearly proved himself today – to some extent, in ways that he still didn't fully understand. Now all he wanted to think about was a hot drink and a warm blanket.

CHAPTER 11

DEBUT DAY

When Erling got the call from one of his friends in the reserve team, the news caught him by surprise. Bryne's first team manager Gaute Larsen was out, and Coach Berntsen would be taking over.

A few hours later, his phone buzzed again. This time, it was Coach Berntsen himself.

'Hi, Erling,' he said, sounding tired from what must have been a long, exhausting day. 'I'm guessing you've heard the news by now?'

'Yes, big news travels fast!' Erling replied. 'Congrats, Coach. I'm really pleased for you and I know you're going to crush it. Hopefully this means we'll get to work together again one day.'

'Well, that's part of the reason for my call. You've blown everyone away with your performances for the reserves – not just the goals but the work ethic and the maturity. I'm sure there were already plans to get you involved in the first team squad but I'm going to be speeding that up. You can count on it.'

Erling grinned. That sounded great. 'Thanks for always believing in me, Coach. I'll be ready.'

Sure enough, within weeks, Coach Berntsen had promoted Erling to the first team squad, where he quickly adjusted to the uptick in quality. He sensed that some of the older Bryne players might not be thrilled to have the latest 'young hotshot' from the academy on board, but Alfie had predicted that. 'Don't let it bother you,' his dad had advised him. 'The only way to win them over is to show you're willing to work just as hard as them. Then your talent will take over from there.'

It only took two days of shooting drills for the occasional frown to turn into excited whispers. Erling was on fire. Left foot, right foot – it really didn't matter. Every shot was a rocket. He finished the session with a thumping left-footed shot that crashed off the underside of the crossbar and bounced into the net. The goalkeeper just stood still like a statue.

Coach Berntsen put an arm round Erling's neck. 'Go easy on our keeper,' he said, laughing. 'At least leave him a bit of confidence for the weekend.'

Before the start of one training session, Erling was already changed and doing keepy-ups on the pitch. Coach Berntsen spotted him and walked over. 'Glad we've got a quiet moment before everyone gets out here,' he said. 'I just wanted to be the one to tell you that you'll be named in the squad to play Ranheim this weekend. We're going to start easing you into some games off the bench, but this is a huge step and so well deserved.'

Erling tried to play it cool but quickly dropped the pretence. He felt his heart beating faster than ever. 'Can't wait, Coach.'

That Sunday, he went through his usual routine, even though he knew there was a real chance that he wouldn't play a single minute. He joined the rest of the substitutes as they warmed up, sidestepping along the touchline while keeping a close eye on the game.

With Bryne losing 1–0, Coach Berntsen motioned for Erling to start getting ready, signalling with his hand that he would be coming on in five minutes. Erling nodded with what he hoped looked like confidence. Inside, his stomach was doing somersaults.

That night, the milestone would sink in more – making his debut before he had even turned sixteen! – but in that moment his main focus was creating an equaliser. Or, even better, scoring one. Wearing a black Number 19 shirt, he jogged onto the pitch and headed over to the right wing.

The nerves disappeared instantly as he got involved in the action. First, he spun away and raced onto a long, floated pass. He skipped past one defender but his cross was easily cleared. He looked like Bryne's biggest threat, finding room again on the right minutes later and almost squeezing a cross to the back post.

It was a bright start and even Erling was surprised at how normal it all felt. His eyes lit up when the ball bounced to him at the edge of the box. For a split second, he pictured curling in a dream goal, but the

Ranheim defence closed in to block his shot.

At the final whistle, even the 1–0 loss couldn't take the shine off Erling's big day. 'I'll admit that I never expected to be sending on a fifteen-year-old for a first team game,' Coach Berntsen said back in the dressing room as the players sat down to digest the result. 'Erling, congratulations on your debut. Can't wait to see what you'll do next.'

The players all cheered, setting aside the disappointment of the scoreline.

Before long, Erling became one of the first names on Coach Berntsen's teamsheet and his consistent performances had scouts across the country (and elsewhere in Europe) paying close attention. As he headed off for a summer break, it was no secret that Erling was a young man in demand.

'At Bryne, we're so proud of everything you've achieved, but equally we want to nudge you forward to the next challenge,' Coach Berntsen explained. 'We've received a great offer from Molde that will give you the chance to test yourself at the next level. What do you think?'

Erling paused, unsure what to say. 'That sounds exciting,' he eventually replied. 'But Bryne is all I've ever known. My head is saying it's a great opportunity, even if my heart is struggling with the idea of leaving this club, and my family, behind.'

'Well, you don't have to decide anything yet. Just give it some thought and we can talk again tomorrow.'

As soon as that call ended, Erling called his parents. Luckily, they were at home together and Alfie turned on speakerphone so they could both hear.

'Mum, Dad, I just got a call from Coach Berntsen.'

Erling stopped to find the right words.

'You're leaving us in suspense!' Alfie said. 'What did he say?'

'Basically, Molde have made a bid to sign me. He wanted to get my reaction to that.'

'And…' Alfie replied, trying to nudge his son along.

'Nothing yet. Am I silly for wanting some time to think it over?'

There was a brief silence and Erling could picture his parents looking at each other while deciding how to answer that.

'Molde is a great club,' Alfie finally said. 'Ole Gunnar Solskjær is the boss there these days and he's a good guy. Just say the word and I can give him a call to get a bit more information. This is the kind of move that could really launch your career. But it has to be what you want. From the very beginning, we've always said that we'll support you all the way with your football as long as you're happy.'

'What's holding you back?' Gry Marita asked.

'Honestly, I'm not sure. Maybe it's the idea of moving away. Maybe it's a fear of not being good enough. I guess I just wanted more time to be absolutely sure before I gave a final answer.'

'There's nothing wrong with that,' Gry Marita replied. 'But believe in yourself. Your dad and I certainly do. This type of opportunity doesn't come up very often. I'd just hate for you to have regrets over it.'

Erling nodded. 'Okay, thanks. I'm going to sleep on it and see how I feel in the morning.'

The next morning, with a clear head, Erling sat at the end of his bed and went over the pros and cons again. By the time he was done, it felt like an easier decision. He wanted to take this chance.

Erling called Coach Berntsen to confirm that he was interested in a move to Molde, and the deal was soon finalised.

'We're going to really miss you,' said Coach Berntsen. 'I'm over-the-moon happy for you, though. One day, Bryne is just going to be one small part of the Erling Haaland story, but I've loved every minute of it.'

CHAPTER 12

TOP
TUNES

'Ils sont les meilleurs. Sie sind die Besten. These are the champions.'

The song caused Erling to stir suddenly in his bed and he instinctively reached out for his phone. He pressed the 'Snooze' button for his alarm and the Champions League music stopped, giving him a few more minutes before he had to start his preparations for the Norway Under-17s game that afternoon.

'What was that?!' a sleepy voice suddenly asked, and Erling remembered that he was sharing the room with teammate Eman Markovic.

'Oh sorry, Eman!' Erling said, rubbing his eyes.

'That's my alarm. Got to dream big!'

Across the room, Eman sat up and grinned. 'The Champions League anthem? Seriously? Only you would have that as your alarm!'

'Come on!' Erling replied. 'If that song doesn't get you fired up to start the day, nothing will. It's legendary.'

'Uh-huh,' Eman replied.

'Okay, let's try this game that I play with my cousin. Close your eyes.'

'That's what I was doing until your lovely alarm went off!' Eman said, pretending to be angry. He closed his eyes anyway.

'Now I'm going to play the song again. What's the first Champions League memory that comes to your mind?'

The anthem blared again from Erling's phone.

Eman stayed quiet, letting the anthem get into its second verse. 'Sergio Ramos,' he said suddenly. 'Late-minute header against Atlético in the final.'

'I should have known you'd go for a Real Madrid goal,' Erling said. 'But that's a good choice. It doesn't get much more dramatic than that. Mine is Zlatan, of course – for PSG against Anderlecht. That absolute rocket into the top corner to complete his hat-trick.'

'How do you remember all of those details?' Eman asked, shaking his head in amazement.

'That tournament is so special to me. It's where the biggest stars really make their name.'

'It's amazing to think that in a few years something like the Champions League could actually be within reach,' Eman said. 'One or two good games in front of the right scouts and suddenly a path to a big club opens up.' He got out of bed and opened the curtains. 'I wonder if the person who wrote the song ever imagined it would last this long.'

'When you see the players lining up for the anthem, you can see on their faces that the song gets them every time. It's a reminder at the start of every Champions League game that they are the best of the best.'

Erling and Eman joined the rest of the squad in the hotel lobby, ready for a quick breakfast then a team meeting. Both of them expected to be in the starting line-up, but it was never a sure thing when the coaches wanted the chance to evaluate as many players as possible in these friendlies.

In the makeshift changing room, the coaches handed out the kits and Erling took charge of setting up some music to get everyone pumped up for the game. As he pulled out his mini speakers and scanned his phone for the playlist he wanted, a few of his teammates started humming. Then a few more joined in. Then the whole squad joined in. They were humming a song he knew very well: the Champions League anthem.

Erling stopped scrolling through his phone and burst out laughing. He looked over at Eman. 'You told them already?!'

Eman giggled and shrugged. 'I couldn't resist, buddy!'

Music, in general, was often on Erling's mind these days, and he didn't hesitate when he saw the chance to create a music video of his own. Teaming up with friends to form the band Flow Kingz, he surprised his whole family by launching a rap video that grew in popularity as Erling continued to shine on the pitch.

Of course, the video was like a gift to his teammates

who were soon doing impressions of Erling's rapping and setting it up on loop in the dressing room. 'I know you're just jealous of my voice,' he said, playing along with the joke.

On his way to the team cafeteria, his phone buzzed with a text from Astor. It was a short message. 'Yikes, stick to football, bro!' Erling laughed to himself as he grabbed a tray and checked out the menu.

CHAPTER 13

GOING IT ALONE

As Erling settled into his new routine at Molde, there was a lot to take in. Sure, he hadn't left the country, but he had swapped the south for the north, with his friends and family in Bryne many hours away. Even though he knew his way around the kitchen and had been drilled by his parents on how to take care of his laundry, it was a big shift for a quiet sixteen-year-old.

When Gry Marita had told Erling that she would sleep better knowing that he could wash his clothes, he had laughed and rolled his eyes. Now, he wished she was with him to help with the first few months.

But he wanted to give himself every chance to become a professional footballer. The football pitch was a safe space, free from homesickness, and Erling put all his energy into becoming a more polished striker.

Molde eased him into the first team gently, with manager Ole Gunnar Solskjær keeping a close eye on him in training. Though Erling was itching for more playing time, he understood that the physicality and speed of the country's top division would take some getting used to for a teenager. 'I've just got to take the chances when I get them,' he told Astor during one of their weekly catch-up phone calls. 'That might be in cup games, it might be in the last few minutes of league games, or even in the reserves.'

Erling got the news he was hoping for at the end of a morning training session. 'You put in a great shift out there again today,' Ole told him, patting Erling on the back. 'It's been great seeing you putting all the pieces together over the last few weeks. You've earned your shot and you're going to be starting in the cup this week.'

As he listened, Erling beamed. 'Thanks, coach. I won't let you down.'

That cup tie pitted Molde against Volda TI, and

Erling took a deep breath to calm himself as he pulled on the 'Haaland 30' shirt. It was end-to-end action from the first whistle and that meant plenty of opportunities for clever movement and quick counter-attacking. Erling darted towards the near post for one first-half chance but his shot was deflected wide. He put his hands on his head. So close!

At half-time, the message was clear. 'Throw everything at them in the first fifteen minutes,' Ole said. 'We're getting into great positions but make that final pass count.'

Early in the second half, Molde won the ball back and got another chance in a 3 v 3 situation. Erling pulled over to the left and burst into the box. 'Slide it through!' he yelled, pointing to where he wanted the ball.

The pass arrived right on time. Erling took two quick touches to set up the angle and then a third to drill a low shot through the goalkeeper's legs. The net rippled.

Goooooooooooooooooooooaaaaaaaaaaaaaaaallllllllllllll llllllllll!!!!!!!!!!!!!!!!!!!

There was no big celebration for Erling – just a casual arm in the air. But it meant a lot to get his first goal for Molde.

After going 2–0 up, Molde let their guard down and suddenly it was 2–2. Erling, having been subbed off, watched nervously from the bench and let out a sigh of relief when Molde hit back for a 3–2 win. Back in the dressing room, Ole was quick to point out the second-half lapses in concentration but finished on a positive note, presenting Erling with the match ball to mark his first goal for the club.

'Woooooooooo,' Erling's teammates cheered. Before he knew it, three bottles of water appeared out of nowhere and were tipped over his head, followed by sweaty hugs.

But Erling wasn't satisfied with a goal in a rare cup appearance. He knew that the next major step was earning a regular place in the team. With every training session, he built a better understanding with the midfielders and other strikers.

Erling got another chance away to Viking FK. With the score locked at 2–2 and Viking down to ten men, he knew that he could exploit tired legs with the right service. A chipped pass over the top sparked a late breakaway through the middle, and Erling sprinted forward in support. As the ball was played across to him, Erling didn't even need a touch to steady himself. He just took the shot first time, placing it confidently into the bottom corner with his left foot.

Goooooooooooooooooooaaaaaaaaaaaaaaaaallllllllllllll lllllllllllll!!!!!!!!!!!!!!!!!!!!

He celebrated in front of the Viking fans as boos rained down on him. As he high-fived his teammates at the final whistle, Erling felt the joy of being the match-winner.

As he reflected on his first season with Molde, Erling was disappointed to finish with just four goals, but his coaches were quick to remind him of all the improvements in his game. He was stronger, better with his back to goal, better in the air and, at still only seventeen, he had time on his side.

His coaches weren't the only ones impressed with his progress. Word was spreading across Europe, with a growing list of suitors lining up for discussions with

Molde. At the front of that line was Red Bull Salzburg in Austria, a club with a strong reputation for helping young players reach their full potential.

With an attractive deal on the table, it would have been tough for Molde to stand in Erling's way. As a compromise, Salzburg agreed that Erling would spend another season honing his skills in Norway before making the move – an arrangement that left everyone with a positive feeling.

'This is all happening so fast,' Erling told his parents on the night that the transfer was announced. 'But it's going to be another great adventure.'

'Plus, you get another year to fire Molde up the table,' Alfie said. 'By the time you put on the Salzburg shirt for the first time, you'll be an even more complete player.'

CHAPTER 14

SHINING WITH SOLSKJÆR

As Erling sat down with the rest of the Molde squad at the team hotel and buttered his plate of toast, something felt different. Maybe he was imagining it, but he had a sense that it was going to be a special day. Molde were facing Brann, the league leaders, and there would be even more eyes on him. He lived for these moments.

His second season with Molde was already off to a better start than his first, with more clinical finishing and a better understanding with his teammates. Up front, he was usually linking with Fredrik Aursnes and Petter Strand who both played with the same relentless energy that Erling did – and the goals were flowing.

An offseason with Alfie and the rest of the family had made a real difference, and it helped that his next steps were already mapped out with the move to Salzburg arranged for the start of the next season. At first, it had felt strange to sign that deal then stick around at Molde for another year, but that feeling quickly wore off.

Most of all, his body was now better prepared to handle physical first-team football. With a combination of a careful diet and hours in the gym, Erling was transformed from a skinny kid into a powerful young man. His teammates noticed the change immediately, giving him the nickname 'Manchild' and feeling the effects in training as Erling's extra strength made it impossible to knock him off the ball.

That afternoon in Brann, Erling's good vibe carried on through the warm-up as he pinged shots into the bottom corner. Even when he was supposed to be giving the goalkeepers some catching practice, he struck the ball sweetly.

It only took a few minutes for Erling to notice that he had the pace to get behind the Brann defence, and

he stayed close to the last defender ready to pounce.
Fredrik leapt to flick on a long ball and suddenly Erling
was through on goal. As the goalkeeper hesitated,
Erling made up his mind in a flash. He got to the ball
first, touched it to the side and then stroked a calm
shot into the empty net.

*Goooooooooooooooooooooaaaaaaaaaaaaaaaaalllllllllllllll
llllllllllllll!!!!!!!!!!!!!!!!!!!!*

'Let's go!' he shouted as Fredrik and Petter wrapped
him in hugs. 'We're just as good as these guys.'

That early goal rocked Brann, and Erling could
sense the panic. A looping pass arrowed towards the
far corner flag, giving him another chance to show
his pace. Erling reached the ball first but there was
no chance of a shot from that angle. Then one of the
Brann defenders lunged in – and that was just the
small opening Erling needed. He flicked the ball away
from the lunge and raced through on goal. He took a
quick glance at the goal, steadied himself and placed a
left-footed shot past the goalkeeper.

*Goooooooooooooooooooooaaaaaaaaaaaaaaaaalllllllllllllll
llllllllllllll!!!!!!!!!!!!!!!!!!!!*

Two minutes later, more disastrous Brann defending put another chance on a plate for Erling. He could hardly believe his luck when a clearing header was badly misjudged by two Brann players. As the ball bounced loose, Erling darted behind the defence, rounded the goalkeeper and passed the ball into the net, just like he had for his first goal.

Goooooooooooooooooooaaaaaaaaaaaaaaaaalllllllllllllll llllllllllll!!!!!!!!!!!!!!!!!!!

'A hat-trick in fifteen minutes!' Fredrik said, laughing as they jogged back to the halfway line. 'You're destroying them.'

'Manchild strikes again!' Petter chimed in.

'I guess it's just my day today,' Erling replied, with a wink.

It soon got even better as Molde won a penalty and Erling grabbed the ball. He gave himself a five-step run-up and took a deep breath. When the referee blew the whistle, he stepped up confidently and sent the goalkeeper the wrong way.

Goooooooooooooooooooaaaaaaaaaaaaaaaaalllllllllllllll llllllllllll!!!!!!!!!!!!!!!!!!!

At half-time, Ole was waiting for Erling on the touchline. 'Wow!' a stunned Ole said, shrugging his shoulders to show that he was lost for words in describing that first half.

Proving himself against a top team like Brann gave Erling huge confidence and really put him on the map in Norway. Unlike his first season when he never quite seemed to be in the right place at the right time, now he was going into games expecting to score. By the end of the season, he had scored sixteen goals.

'You can do anything you set your mind to,' Ole said as he and Erling sat in his office for their end-of-season chat. 'Just look at your growth over the past year. I know a thing or two about scoring goals in big games, and you're ready to take this next step at Salzburg.'

Erling smiled. He knew Ole was right. His time at Molde had been an incredible learning experience, but his move to Salzburg could transform his game at an even faster speed.

As he started to organise his clothes and think about where he would live in Salzburg, he received an invitation for a video call with Salzburg's newly appointed manager Jesse Marsch for later in the week. That eased some of Erling's nerves about the move – it would be nice to make that connection in advance.

The call started with Erling and Jesse, who said all the right things about working together and competing for trophies, and then a few extra visitors logged in. Jesse introduced Erling to Takumi Minamino and Hee-Chan Hwang, two of Salzburg's attackers who would be playing alongside Erling in a few months' time.

Erling felt packed with more energy and enthusiasm after the call, feeling more certain than ever that he was making the right move for his career. Now he just needed to figure out how to fit all of his boots into the suitcase!

CHAPTER 15

ON CLOUD NINE

A chance to play for Norway in the Under-20 World Cup was a dream come true for Erling, prompting calls to all his friends and family. But as he trudged into the meeting room at the team hotel after the first week of the tournament, the excitement had mostly worn off. He sat down next to teammates Jens Petter Hauge and Kristian Thorstvedt, who both looked as disappointed as he was.

Norway had lost their first two games, against Uruguay and New Zealand, and that meant they would be making an early exit from the tournament. All that was left was a final group game against Honduras.

Coach Johansen walked to the front of the room

and the conversations stopped. 'None of us wanted to be in this position, but keep your heads up. We're still playing for our country and the Norway shirt. Let's at least end on a high note.'

By the end of the meeting, Erling felt better and he could see that his teammates were ready to put in an improved performance.

'I'm counting the minutes,' Erling told Alfie on the phone that night. 'We'll be a different team. You'll see.'

As he walked onto the pitch, Erling took a deep breath and looked around the stadium. The hairs on the back of his neck stood on end throughout the national anthem, and he clapped his hands excitedly as he stood on the edge of the centre circle ready for kick-off. 'Let's go, boys!'

Erling was in the middle of the action from the very start, closing down defenders and getting the Norway fans up out of their seats. Inside the first ten minutes, Jens broke away on the left wing and immediately looked up to ping the ball across the box. Erling was already a step ahead of his marker and the cross was perfect. He side-footed a first-time shot past the goalkeeper.

Gooooooooooooooooooooaaaaaaaaaaaaaaaaalllllllllllllll
llllllllllllll!!!!!!!!!!!!!!!!!!!!!

What a start! Erling had an extra spring in his step now and he could see the nerves on the Honduras defenders' faces every time he made a run. Another ball looped over the top of the defence and Erling peeled away to make space. He cushioned the pass with one touch and then hammered an unstoppable shot into the back of the net.

Gooooooooooooooooooooaaaaaaaaaaaaaaaaalllllllllllllll
llllllllllllll!!!!!!!!!!!!!!!!!!!!!

'This is more like it!' he yelled as Jens and Kristian raced over to celebrate.

Erling completed his hat-trick before half-time. He used his pace to latch onto a through ball and touch it past the goalkeeper before being tripped to the ground. Penalty! Erling was up in a flash to grab the ball and place it on the spot. No-one was taking this chance away from him. He carefully marked out his run-up, then stroked the spot-kick calmly into the bottom corner, sending the goalkeeper the wrong way.

Goooooooooooooooooooooaaaaaaaaaaaaaaaalllllllllllll lllllllllll!!!!!!!!!!!!!!!!!!!!!

Before half-time, Erling added a fourth goal with another thumping shot. Coach Johansen high-fived Erling as he walked into the dressing room. 'Terrific work, Erling,' he said. 'You're ripping them apart with your movement.'

In the second half, the chances kept coming as Honduras continued to fade. Erling tucked away a low shot for his fifth goal, reacted fastest in a goalmouth scramble for his sixth and added a tap-in for his seventh. 'Wow, you are in ruthless form today!' Jens said. 'I keep expecting you to score with every touch.'

There was still time for Erling to score his eighth and ninth goals of the game just to put the icing on the cake. He was hitting the ball so sweetly and the ninth goal, in particular, rocketed into the net.

The final score was 12–0 to Norway. With the match ball under his arm, he headed off the pitch with a huge grin on his face. 'I just wish we'd found this kind of form in the other group games,' he said to Kristian as they changed into their Norway tracksuits.

'We'll never know how far we might have gone.'

Still, it was a game that Erling would never forget. As he kept an eye on the rest of the tournament from home, it caught him by surprise when he was announced as the World Cup's top scorer. Amid all the questions and spotlight around Norway's poor results during the tournament, it had slipped his mind.

'That's not the trophy I wanted this summer,' he told Astor. 'But I'll take it.'

As Erling returned to Salzburg ready for his first season in Austria, he immediately got the sense that his nine-goal masterclass had sent scouts from all over the world racing off to file their glowing reports. Sure, he would face sterner tests in the months ahead, but there was no denying the quality of his finishing and the smoothness of his runs.

His agent, Mino Raiola, said it best. 'You're really on the fast-track now, Erling.'

CHAPTER 16

LEADING NORWAY'S NEW ERA

Before the 2019–20 season was even in full swing, Erling's country came calling again. He had been representing Norway through the youth teams for years, but none of that prepared him for the emotions of his first call-up to the senior team.

His phone buzzed as he sat outside on a sunny August afternoon, resting his aching legs after a morning session at the Salzburg training ground. Erling glanced at the screen and saw a number he didn't recognise. For a second, he considered leaving it to go to voicemail, but something made him decide to pick up. 'Hello?'

'Hi, Erling,' said a voice that he vaguely recognised.

'Hope I'm catching you at a good moment. It's Lars Lagerbäck.'

Erling gently tapped his fist against his head. The Norway national team manager. That's why he knew the voice. They had met several times over the past year.

'Hi, how are you?' he replied.

'I'm doing well,' said Lars. 'It's a busy week so I've only got a few minutes. I just wanted to give you some news personally. You'll be in the senior team squad when it gets announced later today.'

Erling felt his legs turn to jelly. Did he really just say 'senior team'? It was a moment he had imagined many times, but now he couldn't find any words to say.

'Congratulations,' Lars continued, sensing that this was big, overwhelming news for Erling, 'It's no secret that you've been destined to join the Norway senior squad for many years, but I know the Norwegian FA has been determined not to pile too much pressure on your shoulders until you're ready. We all think that moment is now.'

'I don't know what to say,' Erling mumbled. 'This is a dream for me. I love playing for Norway and I can't wait to help get us back on the map.'

'That's what we're pushing for too, but I just want you to understand that this is going to be a journey – and no-one is expecting you to be the saviour overnight. As the Norwegian FA said to me, the past twenty years have been tough. Our chances of reaching Euro 2020 are hanging in the balance, but overall we just need to start taking steps in the right direction again.'

Erling thought back to the stories that Alfie used to tell him about playing for Norway and taking on the best teams in the world. As he sat there, still digesting his big news, he realised that he didn't have any memories of Norway in a major tournament in his lifetime.

'I'll leave you to let your family know,' Lars said. 'I'm sure they'll be thrilled. But please just keep it to a small group of people for now. I'd rather wait until the squad is officially announced before fielding questions from reporters.'

After ending the call with Lars, Erling scrolled over to call his parents, then paused. He stood up and walked around the garden, with his mind racing through all kinds of thoughts and memories: seeing his name on the back on the Norway shirt, meeting the rest of the squad, wondering whether he would be good enough at full international level.

He gave himself fifteen minutes to run through all of those topics, then he took a deep breath and phoned his parents. Predictably, it was an emotional call. He could hear his mum fighting back tears and even his dad seemed choked up by the news.

'That's going to be a night you'll never forget, son,' Alfie said. 'Put us down for as many tickets as you can get!'

Erling laughed. 'Yeah, we might need our own section once the ticket requests start pouring in.' He was already thinking about how many of his old friends and teammates would soon be in touch – most to congratulate him and probably a few to plead for tickets.

Any concerns about how his call-up would be

received by the rest of the Norway squad were immediately put to rest. Some players texted him as soon as Lars announced that Erling would be moving into the senior squad, while others were quick to welcome him when the players gathered to discuss the game plans for facing Malta and Sweden.

There were no guarantees that Erling would be in the starting line-up for either of these games. In fact, he knew the likeliest scenario was being named among the substitutes. But after a couple of training sessions, Erling could see that he belonged at this level and was already standing out among the current squad. He could see Lars and the other coaches watching closely and taking notes. It certainly helped that he ended the first session with a fierce volley into the top corner that left everyone murmuring in amazement.

In the final meeting before the Malta game, Lars went through the team that would start this important qualifying game. Erling sat nervously and then tried to contain his excitement when he heard his name called out as one of the strikers.

When the squad arrived in the dressing room,

Erling saw his 'Haaland 23' shirt already hanging from a locker in the far corner. While his teammates either checked their phones or started changing for the warm-up, he couldn't resist lifting the hanger off the hook, taking a closer look at the shirt he was about to wear and taking a few photos as souvenirs.

The national anthem was another proud moment, helping to make everything sink in. He was making his international debut, on home soil in Oslo, and he was still just nineteen. Best of all, he knew his parents, brother, sister and countless others were in the stadium roaring him on.

He quickly showed the Malta defenders that he wasn't afraid, challenging for headers and brushing off their attempts to hold him back. Norway were 2–0 up by half-time and, while he would have loved to be one of the scorers, Erling was enjoying every minute of it. As with so many other debuts in his short career so far, he was fitting right in.

When he was replaced in the second half, Erling turned to clap to the crowd and got deafening applause in return. He had read the stories during the week about this being the dawn of a new era for Norway and it felt like a good start. Lars shook his hand as he walked towards the bench. 'Terrific debut, Erling,' he said. 'The first of many caps for your country.'

Lars picked a more defensive formation for the trip to Sweden, but Erling still got a short appearance as a substitute. A 1–1 draw was another good result, and he had learned so much from his first week with the senior squad. As Erling returned to Salzburg to put his focus back on his club, his confidence was soaring and his football 'to do' list was now a little shorter. 'What next?' he thought to himself.

CHAPTER 17

OWNING THE BIG STAGE

As Erling stood in the tunnel, he could already hear the Salzburg fans. This was the moment he had been waiting for, and clearly the fans were just as excited as he was. In less than ten minutes, Erling would be making his Champions League debut against Belgian club Genk. In some ways, he felt like the Champions League had been part of his life forever. He had watched so many special European games on TV growing up, seeing his heroes' names being written into the history books. Now, it was his turn.

Suddenly, the line was moving. Erling could see the referee up ahead. There were the familiar sounds of boots clattering on the ground as the players walked down the tunnel towards the pitch. Erling stepped from the tunnel onto the edge of the pitch and the electric atmosphere almost took his breath away.

'So this is what a Champions League night feels like,' he said quietly to himself.

He lined up with his teammates and waved to the little boy who had been paired up with him on the way out. Looking into the crowd, he saw a sea of red shirts and a flare going off in one corner of the stadium. He was so busy taking in all the sights that it almost made him jump when the Champions League anthem blasted out on the loudspeakers.

Erling couldn't help but smile to himself. The anthem. His anthem. '*Ils sont les meilleurs. Sie sind die Besten. These are the champions.*'

Somehow, the crowd seemed even louder now, and Erling was ready to feed off that energy. As he knocked the ball back and forth with Takumi, he spotted Jesse calling him over for some last-minute instructions.

'Ready to make a flying start?' Jesse asked, as Erling leaned closer to hear over the noise of the fans. 'Pressure them early on and stay on that last defender.

They're going to be terrified of your pace.'

Erling nodded and smiled.

'And enjoy it!' Jesse added, giving Erling a fist bump. 'You were made for nights like this.'

With Jesse's words sticking in his mind and the crowd screaming their support, Erling felt unstoppable. Salzburg pushed Genk back with an early attack, starting down the left and then cutting back inside. Takumi found a yard of space on the edge of the box and Erling immediately darted on a little diagonal run, leaving his defender in the dust. Takumi slipped a quick pass into his stride and Erling arrived right on time, thumping a low shot past the goalkeeper.

Goooooooooooooooooooooaaaaaaaaaaaaaaaaaallllllllllllllll llllllllllllll!!!!!!!!!!!!!!!!!!!!!

Erling raced over to the fans, signalling for them to get even louder. 'I can't hear you!' he screamed, putting a hand behind each ear. Takumi jumped on his back. 'What a rocket!' he shouted.

Genk were rattled. Erling could see it on the players' faces. Every time they gave the ball away, there was panic and finger-pointing. 'Time for a knockout blow,' he whispered to Takumi as they waited for a throw-in.

Erling was everywhere, dropping deeper to help press the ball and then making clever runs behind the full-backs. A long Salzburg clearance sent Hee-Chan on a one-on-one race with a Genk defender. Some players might have stood and watched, waiting to see how the move developed. But Erling was instantly sprinting. Hee-Chan was fast enough to get to the ball first and strong enough to hold off the defender, but he was stumbling and needed to lay the ball off.

'I'm here!' Erling called, straining every muscle to catch up with his teammate. As he fell, Hee-Chan managed to poke the ball to where Erling was charging forward. In a flash, Erling cushioned the pass, opened up his body and curled a left-footed shot into the bottom corner.

Goooooooooooooooooooooaaaaaaaaaaaaaaaaalllllllllllllll lllllllllllll!!!!!!!!!!!!!!!!!!!!

What a move! End-to-end in five seconds. As Erling celebrated again, he turned to point to Hee-Chan. 'That was all you, buddy!' he shouted. 'I just did the easy part.'

On the touchline, Erling could see what the moment meant to Jesse too. His manager looked over and gave him a thumbs up. But Erling wasn't done yet. Genk were falling apart and he could smell more goals. Hee-Chan quickly made it 3–0, before Genk pulled a goal back. For a moment, the crowd was silenced, but the singing and clapping soon got going again.

Again, Salzburg attacked down the left wing. With Genk outnumbered, Erling just concentrated on staying onside. The low cross was perfect and he stretched out his right foot to guide the ball into the net.

Gooooooooooooooooooooaaaaaaaaaaaaaaaaallllllllllllll llllllllllll!!!!!!!!!!!!!!!!!!!

A first-half hat-trick on his Champions League debut! Erling's head was still spinning as he walked off the pitch at half-time. 'If this is all a dream, please don't wake me up,' he said to Takumi as they high-fived.

Genk tightened up their defensive game plan in the second half, but the damage had been done. As the Salzburg fans gave the players a standing ovation at the final whistle, Erling could not recall a better feeling in his short career so far. Now he just needed to find the match ball.

He spotted the referee walking towards the tunnel with the ball tucked under his arm. Even after such a draining game, both physically and emotionally, Erling had enough energy to run across the pitch. 'Ref, hang on a minute,' he called, starting to feel his muscles aching. 'Can I have the ball for my collection?'

For a second, the referee looked confused, then he remembered that Erling had scored a hat-trick. He smiled. 'Of course,' he said, throwing the ball under-arm to Erling. 'Well played tonight.'

He was one of the last players to get back to the dressing room, and he could hear the music and laughter from the corridor. As he walked in, his teammates turned around and the volume went up another level. 'Manchild!' they screamed, wrapping him in hugs and Erling jumped up and down with them.

That Champions League debut was a sign of things to come, as Erling entered the history books with his scoring during the group stage. With goals in his next four Champions League games, he joined Alessandro

Del Piero and Diego Costa as the only players in the history of the competition to score in each of their first five games. Still, it wasn't enough as Salzburg finished third in the group.

In some ways, though, it was short-lived disappointment. Erling had made such a strong start at Salzburg that, according to the rumours, the world's biggest clubs were circling with intent. Still, there was nothing concrete yet. Erling concentrated on giving his all in training but kept track of the latest news via regular calls with Mino. The more he heard, the more one thing already seemed certain: his stop in Salzburg was going to be a brief one.

CHAPTER 18

DORTMUND BOUND

Erling got up from the sofa and paced around the room. 'The number one thing is playing regularly,' he kept saying. 'Otherwise, it's a non-starter for me.' To him, the last two weeks had felt like two years as he met with Alfie, Mino and several others to discuss the different teams that were interested in signing him.

There was undeniably a certain appeal with football giants like Juventus, Real Madrid and Manchester United, but Erling wanted to keep an open mind. Most of all, he wanted to avoid signing a big-money deal that left him sitting on the bench for the next few years.

'Put the possibilities of Juventus, Real and United

aside for now,' Alfie said. 'I get your concerns there. Let's talk about some of the other options. What about Borussia Dortmund?'

Erling was nodding. 'Yes, Dortmund caught my eye too.'

'They seem like an ambitious, well-run club with great fans and lots of young talent already in the squad,' Alfie added. 'You could immediately become the focal point of their attack.'

Further information from Dortmund representatives about the club's future plans made Erling even more excited. From that point, things happened fast. Salzburg and Dortmund hammered out the terms of the transfer and suddenly Erling was putting his signature on a stack of forms to complete the deal. He would be a Dortmund player by January 2020.

'Erling, we're so excited to be bringing you to Dortmund,' explained Michael Zorc, the club's sporting director, as they celebrated the transfer. 'And you're going to be a fan favourite in no time.'

As Erling got settled in Dortmund, Alfie reminded him to be patient. 'Don't forget, you're still nineteen, it's halfway through the season and you're joining a top club with established stars. If it takes a few months for you to make your mark, that's okay.' At the same time, Alfie and Gry Marita knew that it wasn't really in Erling's personality to take a back seat.

From the first training session, Erling brought the same mindset as he had with the senior Norway call-up. He would do whatever the coaches asked him to do, start to bond with his new teammates and let his performances in training do the talking. It certainly helped that he was joining a club brimming with like-minded young stars, and he immediately felt at home.

Dortmund boss Lucien Favre had been quick to make one key introduction ahead of that first training session. Before changing into his kit, Erling was directed to a meeting room, where a youthful face sat next to Lucien.

'Erling Haaland, meet Jadon Sancho,' Lucien said.

Erling leaned across to shake hands.

'As you know, we are big believers in giving young players opportunities to shine in the first team, and that starts with positioning you two to spearhead our attack. We're building a young core that is going to make Dortmund a contender for years to come.'

As it turned out, Erling didn't need to be patient for his chance at all. After watching the newcomer link well with Jadon and team captain Marco Reus all week in training, Lucien had a quiet word with Erling during a brief water break.

'You've slotted in so easily this week,' Lucien said as Erling stopped guzzling from his bottle and turned to face his manager. 'I'm really impressed. We'll get you on the bench for the FC Augsburg game and you'll definitely be involved.'

Erling smiled. 'Thanks, boss. I'm loving it here. Can't wait to get the black-and-yellow shirt on.'

As Erling warmed up during the first half and cracked jokes with the other substitutes, he saw Dortmund struggling to create chances and knew it was the kind of game that he could shake up. For a start, the FC Augsburg defence were playing such a high line and there was often forty yards of inviting green grass for a through ball.

With Dortmund trailing 1–0 at half-time, Erling

wondered how quickly Lucien would turn to his bench. He went through all the normal stretches, wanting to be ready if he got the signal. Lucien gave his starting line-up a chance to make amends but when Dortmund fell behind, 3–1, he motioned to Erling.

'We need some of that Haaland magic to get back into this,' Lucien said.

Erling jogged onto the pitch and immediately stood next to the deepest FC Augsburg defender. Whenever Dortmund won the ball back, he was on the move, either making diagonal runs out to the wings for a long pass, or working on an angled run from a wider position.

As Dortmund played the ball through midfield, it was as if the move was developing in slow motion. Before anyone else, Erling saw the opportunity to curl his run behind the defence and stay onside. He set off sprinting and the pass was inch perfect for his trademark left-footed strike. Erling made sure he felt balanced then fired a shot across the goalkeeper towards the bottom corner. The ball bounced off the inside of the post and into the net.

Goooooooooooooooooooooaaaaaaaaaaaaaaaaallllllllllllllll lllllllllllll!!!!!!!!!!!!!!!!!!!

But there was no time to celebrate. They were still losing. Erling ran to scoop the ball out of the net and sprinted with it back to the halfway line, high-fiving his teammates on the way.

'Keep playing the ball through,' he called. 'There's so much space.'

Sure enough, a long clearance flew over the heads of the FC Augsburg defence and again it became a race to the ball. Jadon and Erling were always going to win that. This time, Jadon reached it first, dribbled round the goalkeeper and netted the equaliser. Erling was the first one to catch up with Jadon over by the corner flag, jumping on his back.

FC Augsburg didn't learn their lesson. With their defenders almost standing on the halfway line, it was an open invitation for Dortmund to float passes over the top. Another diagonal pass sent Thorgan Hazard through on goal. Erling sprinted up in support. 'Here if you need me!' he called. Thorgan knocked the ball around the keeper, then unselfishly cut it back for

Erling to tap into an open net.

Goooooooooooooooooooaaaaaaaaaaaaaaaaalllllllllllllll llllllllllll!!!!!!!!!!!!!!!!!!

What a comeback! Unbelievably, there was still time for Erling to chase another hat-trick. Again, he held his run carefully, knowing that he would easily get to a through ball before any of the defenders. Marco spotted an angle and fed the pass into the gap, sending Erling through for the kind of one-on-one chance that he lived for. There was only going to be one outcome. He tucked his shot under the goalkeeper and watched the net ripple.

Goooooooooooooooooooaaaaaaaaaaaaaaaaalllllllllllllll llllllllllll!!!!!!!!!!!!!!!!!!

A debut hat-trick. Erling's performance dominated the headlines, but he was just as excited by all the midfield creators in the Dortmund squad. He was not going to be short of goalscoring chances in this team.

After such a dominant debut, Erling was a little disappointed to be back on the bench for the next game, but he still made his case to start, scoring twice as a substitute against 1. FC Köln. Another double sunk Union Berlin, and Erling was off to a flying start.

'Seven goals in three games – I think you've got a chance to be a good player one day ☺ ' Astor texted.

The strangest part of Erling's first season at Dortmund was being back in the Champions League just months after being eliminated in the group stage with Salzburg.

He burst out laughing when he got a message from Eman the night before facing PSG. 'I guess when you have the Champions League anthem as your alarm, they let you play in it twice in the same year!'

Given a second chance in the tournament, Erling was determined to take advantage and was delighted to be starting. But the PSG defence kept a close eye on him, denying him the space to make his usual runs.

At half-time, Lucien gave him a pat on the back. 'Keep looking for those runs,' he said. 'I know they're shutting that off, but we only need to get it right once.'

Erling nodded, but he also had another thought. It felt like the kind of game where he would need to find other ways to score.

And that's what he did. Lurking in the box, Erling reacted fastest when the ball bounced off a couple of players. He slid forward and swept the ball into the net. He checked for an offside flag, but the assistant referee had the flag by his side.

Gooooooooooooooooooooaaaaaaaaaaaaaaaaalllllllllllllll llllllllllllll!!!!!!!!!!!!!!!!!!!!

For once, Erling didn't sprint over to the fans. Instead, he sat down on the pitch in a meditation pose as his teammates knelt down to hug him.

Playing against Kylian Mbappé and Neymar, Erling knew that one goal might not be enough to secure a first leg lead. That proved correct when the pair combined for a slick equaliser.

But, even with a young team, Dortmund had been through enough battles to keep their composure in this type of moment. They just went back to playing the game at their pace. A quick breakaway would normally have been the signal for Erling to sprint beyond the last defender for a long through ball, but this time he faked that run and instead darted back to receive the ball to his feet. With the PSG defenders backing off, he dribbled into shooting range and, without hesitation, smashed a shot towards goal from twenty-five yards out. As soon as the ball left his foot, he knew where it was heading. He looked up to see it arrowing into the top corner.

Goooooooooooooooooooooaaaaaaaaaaaaaaaaaalllllllllllllll llllllllllll!!!!!!!!!!!!!!!!!!!

'You don't save those!' Marco screamed, chasing after Erling, who had thrown himself on the ground in celebration. The whole team dived on top of him as Dortmund grabbed a vital first leg lead.

But that joy was replaced with agony in the return leg in France as PSG won 2–0 to edge the tie, causing one of the quietest dressing rooms that Erling could remember. Still, as time passed, he thought more about the bigger picture. This young Dortmund team was going to keep getting stronger.

When Erling watched Bayern Munich take on PSG in that year's Champions League final, he was even more determined to be on that stage. 'One day, that's going to be me,' he said to Astor on their video call as the Bayern players lifted the trophy.

'I'm sure it will be,' Astor said. He had learned a long time ago that when Erling set his mind on something, it usually worked out for him.

CHAPTER 19

THE BEDTIME
ROUTINE

As Erling prepared for his parents to arrive in
Dortmund for a short visit, he walked through his
living room and kitchen once again for a final check.
Everything seemed pretty tidy. 'Good enough,' he
said, grinning. He hoped his tidying would pass his
mum's inspection.

He heard a car pulling into the driveway and
headed to the front door. They were here!

'Welcome!' he said, waving. He was eager to show
his parents around his new home.

Seeing his parents with their hands full, he jogged
out to help, taking a suitcase from Alfie and a couple
of bags from Gry Marita. 'I thought you were only

here for a few days,' he joked, as they carried in all the luggage.

Alfie laughed. 'Well, we've also brought a few of your things. You know, now that you've got this beautiful place, we're reclaiming the space in our garage.'

Erling smiled, remembering how quickly the garage got filled with his football stuff. 'Ah yes, the old kits, the cuttings, the boots…'

'Don't forget the match balls,' Alfie said. 'We've got a big bag of those in the car – and don't worry, they've all still got the notes on them so you remember which hat-trick is which.'

'Even the most recent ones?' he asked.

Gry Marita nodded. 'Yes, whoever is in charge of tracking down those match balls seems to do a very good job of remembering to mail them to us!'

Erling gave her his best 'I'm sorry, forgive me' face.

Over the next few days, Erling took a trip down memory lane, back through some of his best moments on a football pitch. 'You weren't joking when you said you'd brought a lot of the match balls!' he said, turning to Alfie. 'There's fifteen of them here.'

'And we'll be glad to send the rest very soon,' Gry Marita added, laughing.

Erling reached for the next one. The ball from his hat-trick against Genk in the Champions League. 'This was a special one,' he said, talking to himself. He bounced the ball a couple of times on the wooden floor. 'That night, I felt like I couldn't miss.'

After his parents' visit, Erling moved the balls upstairs to his room and put three of his favourite ones on the bed next to him. That night, he fell asleep watching a film – and woke up with a fright as he rolled over and landed on the balls, sending them bouncing off the bed and into his wardrobe.

Once he told the story to a couple of his teammates, it quickly became legendary. 'Erling Haaland – he's so dedicated that he sleeps next to a football,' Jadon said, putting on his best news reporter voice.

'Go ahead, make fun of me,' Erling replied. 'As long as I keep scoring hat-tricks, I don't care.'

'Well, you'll need a bigger bed then,' Marco joined in, giggling.

'Is there a certain type of pillow that's best for

footballs?' Jadon joked. 'You want them to be comfortable, I'm sure.'

Erling shook his head, pretending to be angry. When Jadon wasn't looking, he chipped the ball gently in his direction, dropping it perfectly on the back of his friend's head.

Jadon turned, laughing. 'I guess I deserved that.'

In truth, Erling was happy to give his teammates something to laugh about – even if they were laughing at him. He was starting to see more clearly what his dad had meant all those years ago about the importance of the relationships with his teammates and how those bonds translated to special moments on the pitch.

Dortmund was quickly turning into a home away from home.

CHAPTER 20

UNLEASHING "THE TERMINATOR"

'Ah, the sweet smell of preseason!' Erling said as he and Jadon flicked the ball back and forth on the training pitch.

'Before all the pressure starts, you mean?' Jadon replied, grinning.

'Yeah, something like that! But I think we're ready for it this year. We've got the talent to be fighting for all the big trophies.'

'With you, me and Marco getting a full preseason together, we're going to be even better this year.'

'You two are so good at creating the chances,' Erling said, then he grinned. 'Plus, every now and again, I'll try to set you up as well.'

Jadon laughed. 'We all know you've got the easy job.'

Once training started, it was all business. Last season was forgotten. Now, it was all about moving forward and closing the gap on Bayern Munich.

Lucien walked the players through what he expected and explained some of the new ideas that he hoped would make Dortmund even stronger. Erling nodded as he listened. He couldn't remember a time when he was more excited about the start of a season.

It also made him smile to look around the meeting room and, after so many years of being the baby-faced youngster, see players who were younger than him. Jude Bellingham and Gio Reyna were both seventeen, and Erling had already started teasing them about his availability as a senior player if they ever needed a 'veteran' for advice.

When the calendar finally flipped to the first game of the season against Borussia Mönchengladbach, Erling felt sharper and stronger than ever. His black-and-yellow Dortmund shirt looked better than ever too. As he stood in the tunnel, across from the Mönchengladbach players, he just stared straight ahead avoiding eye contact with anyone. He was in his zone – and that meant trouble for Bundesliga defenders.

It was a nice feeling to see fans back in the stadium too after months of empty stands due to global health concerns. Erling clapped to the crowd as he walked onto the pitch. Even though the stands weren't at full capacity, the stadium seemed loud after months of being empty.

Lucien's final words to the team had been 'to play without fear in the Mönchengladbach half' – and the players delivered. Jude set up Gio for a neat opening goal, then Erling took over in the second half.

When the referee pointed to the penalty spot after a video review, Erling grabbed the ball. 'Are you sure you don't want to let me take it?' Jadon asked, grinning.

Erling laughed. 'So kind of you to offer, but I've got this.'

He placed the ball on the spot confidently and stepped back to look at the goal. Then with a few quick steps and a momentary pause, he curled the penalty into the bottom corner as the goalkeeper dived the wrong way.

Goooooooooooaaaaaaaallllllllllllllllllllll!!!!!!!!!!!!!!!!

He ran over to the fans, pumping his fists. He was off the mark for the 2020–21 season.

'Maybe I can have the next one then,' Jadon joked as they jogged back to the halfway line.

With Mönchengladbach pushing forward, Lucien was up on the touchline, motioning for the defenders to look for the long ball if Dortmund won the ball back. Sure enough, a Mönchengladbach corner was cleared to Jadon and the break was on.

Jadon raced away down the left wing, and Erling was sprinting too. 'I'm with you!' he yelled as he caught up with his friend. As they closed in on the penalty area, Jadon slid through a clever pass and Erling hammered a shot past the goalkeeper.

Goooooooooooooooooooooaaaaaaaaaaaaaaaaaalllllllllllllll lllllllllllll!!!!!!!!!!!!!!!!!!!!

'What a move!' Erling shouted as he ran over to Jadon. He was still catching his breath.

This was the kind of football that Erling loved. Dortmund were electric on the counter-attack, with pace, vision and movement. Erling knew if he just made the right runs, the ball would be there.

And he had an even more ruthless performance up his sleeve for a trip to Hertha Berlin. With Dortmund trailing 1–0 at half-time, the frustration was written all over Lucien's face. 'Wake up, lads. We need more movement and more energy. Get back to playing our football.'

Within three minutes, Erling had turned the game around. First, he reacted fastest to a low cross, poking the ball over the line.

Goooooooooooooooooooooaaaaaaaaaaaaaaaaalllllllllllllll llllllllllll!!!!!!!!!!!!!!!!!!!!

He grabbed the ball and hurried back to the halfway line. 'Let's go!' he shouted.

With the Hertha Berlin defence still reeling, Erling got free again. This time, the chance was much tougher. But he always trusted himself to hit the target on his left foot. He had time for a quick touch and then fired an unsaveable shot into the far corner.

Goooooooooooooooooooooaaaaaaaaaaaaaaaaalllllllllllllll llllllllllll!!!!!!!!!!!!!!!!!!!!

'This is more like it!' Jude yelled, jumping on Erling's back. 'Cracking strike! You're like The

Terminator, just blowing them away.'

'I'm not sure my muscles are that big,' Erling replied, laughing. 'But we're definitely doing some damage. Those centre-backs are shaky so keep looking for the ball over the top.'

Now he was prowling for chances and closing down defenders. He could feel the panic every time he made a quick run. Then Hertha Berlin gave him an unexpected gift. An overhit backpass rolled past one of the centre-backs and Erling was on it in a flash, flying past the retreating defender, rounding the goalkeeper and passing the ball into the net.

Goooooooooooooooooooooaaaaaaaaaaaaaaaaalllllllllllllll llllllllllllll!!!!!!!!!!!!!!!!!!!!!

He couldn't hide his grin as he ran off to celebrate again. 'That's a hat-trick, baby!' he called out as the Hertha Berlin fans booed him.

There was still time for one more. As Jude got the ball thirty yards out, Erling curved his run between two defenders and counted on his teammate to spot it. The pass was threaded through and, in this sort of form, Erling didn't even think about taking a touch to control it. He just swung his left foot and watched the ball fly into the net, almost taking the goalkeeper with it.

Goooooooooooooooooooaaaaaaaaaaaaaaaaallllllllllllllll llllllllllll!!!!!!!!!!!!!!!!!!!

'Magic pass, buddy!' Erling said as he high-fived Jude. Even as someone who had been a teenage sensation himself, Erling sometimes couldn't believe how good Jude already was and how easy he made things look.

When a league representative dropped by a Dortmund training session to present Erling with the Player of the Month trophy, Erling was quick to mention his teammates' hard work. 'I share this with all of them. They just make me look good.'

'Don't listen to him!' Jadon called out, grinning. 'He thinks he's a one-man team.'

The rest of the squad burst out laughing as Erling wagged his finger in an attempt to confirm that Jadon was joking. 'Do you see what I have to deal with every day?!' he said to the league representative who then joined in the laughter.

CHAPTER 21

CHASING THE
EURO 2020 DREAM

Ever since making his debut for the Norway senior team, Erling had been keeping an especially close eye on the Euro 2020 qualifying tables. Like Lars had said at the time, there were no guarantees that the Norwegians would make it to the tournament, but they would give it their best shot. Erling was feeling more and more comfortable as part of the squad – helped, in part, by scoring his first international goal with a clever finish against Austria.

Spain and Sweden held the upper hand in Norway's Euro 2020 qualifying group, but the playoffs offered another route to what seemed likely to be a wide-open tournament. 'If we can't catch the top two, there's a possible safety net for us,' Erling explained to his sister Gabrielle. 'But then we'd have to win a few playoff matchups to clinch a spot.'

A couple of last-minute goals against Spain and Romania kept Norway in contention, but they had to settle for third place and a spot in the playoffs. That path began against Serbia.

'We've shown great character throughout this qualifying run,' Lars told the team as they prepared for the big game. 'Whatever happens tonight, I'm really proud of you all.'

With Erling in red-hot form at Dortmund, it was no surprise to him that Serbia's game plan often involved keeping two defenders close to him. But he was used to that kind of attention from his youth games and he just focused on moving the ball quickly, so that his teammates could take advantage of the extra space.

As the game entered the final ten minutes, Erling could see that there were tired legs on both teams. As a Serbia free kick bounced dangerously in the penalty area, the ball was clipped back across the box. Erling's heart sank as a Serbia midfielder poked the ball into the net. Norway had eight minutes to save themselves.

But Erling refused to give up. He won headers and tackles, and raced to get the ball any time it went out for a throw-in. Every second counted. When Mathias, one of the Norway substitutes, drove forward, Erling peeled away into the penalty area, taking two defenders with him. It opened up space for Mathias to dribble forward and fire a low shot into the bottom corner. They were level!

Extra-time was a step too far, though. Serbia quickly took the lead again – and this time there would be no Norway comeback. Erling slumped to the ground at the final whistle, struggling to believe that the Euro 2020 dream was over for his team, despite all their hard work.

'Great effort, guys,' Lars said, his voice echoing in the quiet dressing room. 'It just wasn't our night. I know this stings now, but use it as motivation for what comes next. We've got World Cup qualifying to prepare for, then the next European Championships. We're building something here and I really believe we're heading in the right direction.'

Erling knew Lars was right, but it was hard not to let the loss linger with the stakes so high. He kept asking himself whether he could have made one better decision or done better with one half-chance. Maybe that would have turned the game in Norway's favour. He would never know.

'Keep moving forward,' Alfie advised him, noticing that his son seemed weighed down by missing out on Euro 2020. 'You'll have plenty more chances to get Norway back to a big tournament and you can see that the fans are already starting to believe in the national team again. Don't lose sight of all the positives from your first year in the national team.'

Erling gave himself a few more hours to dwell on the disappointment, then he put it behind him. Yes, it would be tough to watch the Euros knowing that Norway had been close to making it, but it only added to his motivation to help his country qualify for another major tournament as soon as possible.

In the meantime, it felt like there were big things on the horizon at Dortmund and that needed his full attention.

CHAPTER 22

OVERCOMING OBSTACLES

Back at Dortmund, Erling was showing that his impressive start to the season was no fluke. But just as his confidence and sharpness were reaching all-time highs, he was grounded by a hamstring injury. In a 5 v 5 mini-game at the end of training, he was chasing a pass when he felt a sharp pain in the back of his leg and came to a hobbling stop, putting a hand in the air. Jude and Jadon were the first to run over to see him as he slumped to the ground. 'Just stay still,' Jadon said, putting a head on Erling's shoulder. 'We're calling the physio over.'

Erling smacked his fist against the pitch in frustration as the physio rushed over and strapped ice around his hamstring. He had managed to avoid major injuries in his youth team days, but this one felt bad. 'Maybe the tests will show it's a minor strain,' Gry Marita told him, trying to keep his spirits up while he waited for news.

'I'm keeping my fingers crossed,' Erling replied. 'But it felt like what I always imagined a torn muscle would feel like. Hopefully I'm wrong.'

The Dortmund medical team confirmed Erling's worst fears and made it very clear that he would need to allow the hamstring to heal for at least a month before he could even think about starting some light training. As much as he loved playing FIFA on his PlayStation, the idea of resting the injury at home didn't sound like much fun.

Still, after getting over the initial disappointment, Erling gave his all to the recovery process, completing all the exercises recommended by the Dortmund physios and avoiding the temptation to kick a ball around at home. But he wished he could be on the pitch helping his teammates, especially after some poor results led to Lucien being sacked.

Gradually, he made progress, and he was relieved to be back in the starting line-up in early January. The goals soon started flowing again, just in time for Dortmund's Champions League second round tie against Sevilla.

As the players went through their final preparations in the dressing room in Seville, interim boss Edin Terzić rallied the players. 'I know this season has been rocky at times, but throw all that out of the window and embrace this moment,' he said. 'This is the Champions League. This is the greatest club competition in the world. Go out and put on a show.'

The players jumped up, clapping, high-fiving and cheering. It felt good to get some of the nervous energy out of the way.

As always, the Champions League anthem gave Erling an extra five per cent boost. This was the stage for career-defining performances. He hopped up and down on the edge of the centre circle, ready to fight for every ball.

Even when Sevilla made a flying start and took a 1–0 lead, Erling remained calm. The Dortmund defence had been wobbly lately, but he knew that he, Jadon and Marco could come to the rescue.

First, it was midfielder Mahmoud Dahoud who got Dortmund back on track with a beautiful curling shot. After that, Erling took control of the game, stretching Sevilla with his movement and muscling defenders off the ball.

Erling dropped deeper to collect a pass, then saw he had room to turn and attack. He laid the ball off to Jadon and dashed through the middle for the one-two. Jadon looped a return pass towards him and Erling slid forward to reach it as the goalkeeper flew off his line. But Erling got there first, prodding the ball into the net.

Goooooooooooooooooooooaaaaaaaaaaaaaaaalllllllllllll llllllllllll!!!!!!!!!!!!!!!!!!!

As Jadon and Marco ran over to celebrate, Erling's thoughts went back to all the hard work involved in his recovery from the hamstring injury. It was the chance to get back to moments like scoring in the Champions League that he had used for motivation.

Before half-time, Erling did it again. Dortmund won the ball in midfield and flew forward. Marco dribbled to the edge of the Sevilla box then clipped a pass right into Erling's path. Opening up his body to hit the ball left-footed, Erling whipped a shot into the net.

Goooooooooooooooooooooaaaaaaaaaaaaaaaaaalllllllllllllll lllllllllllll!!!!!!!!!!!!!!!!!!!!

The bus journey back to the team hotel was one of the happiest Erling could remember. 'When we're counter-attacking like that, no one can get near us,' he said, as he and Jadon replayed the goals on his phone.

Dortmund needed Erling's magic again in the second leg, as Sevilla pushed them to the limit. He scored twice in a 2–2 draw to book their place in the quarter-finals.

Edin walked into the dressing room after the post-game interviews and pointed for the music to be turned down. He was holding a sheet of paper in his hand.

'Well done tonight, lads,' Edin said. 'That's a good team we just knocked out. I loved the effort and the poise when things got tense at the end.' The players all clapped.

'Also, a special mention for Erling,' Edin continued,

glancing at the paper. 'Tonight you scored your twentieth Champions League goal in just your fourteenth game. That's the fastest anyone has ever scored twenty goals in this competition. Congratulations, big man.'

Now the clapping turned to cheering and singing. Marco and Jadon grabbed water bottles and started spraying Erling as he tried to take cover behind his towel.

While Dortmund's Champions League journey ended in quarter-final heartbreak against Manchester City, there was a lot to be proud of. Edin gave the players some space with the disappointment still so fresh, but he was quick to remind the team that there was still plenty to play for.

Erling sat quietly at his locker and slowly nodded his head. The Champions League exit hurt, but he was determined to end the season on a high note.

CHAPTER 23

TROPHY TIME

When Dortmund clinched their place in the 2021 DFB-Pokal cup final, Erling was in the middle of all the celebrations. But, as the final inched closer, he saw more and more clearly that the outcome of the final would shape everyone's view of this season. Victory would bring a first major trophy for him, Jadon, Jude and the rest of this young Dortmund core. Defeat would mean they finished the season empty-handed and faced an uncertain summer.

RB Leipzig stood in their way, but Erling felt confident. Dortmund had won both of their league clashes that season and, though Leipzig had the league's best defensive record, Erling knew where the weak spots were.

'This is our moment,' he said to Jadon as they warmed up on the pitch and tried to think of this as just another game. 'We'll have the eyes of the whole country on us today.'

Jadon was nodding while tapping the ball from foot to foot. 'Big-time players show up in big-time games. Today, that's got to be us.'

Despite knowing how important this game was, Erling had felt calm all week. As he expected, the usual nervous energy surfaced as he walked down the tunnel with his teammates but, more than anything, he was just excited.

Jadon got Dortmund off to a dream start. Erling controlled a pass, laid it off and then sprinted towards the box. As defenders crowded around him, it freed up Jadon to go one-on-one on the left wing. He cut inside and curled a screamer into the top corner.

'Big-time player!' Erling shouted as they celebrated by the corner flag.

Jadon winked. 'I can't let you do all the heavy lifting,' he said.

As Edin stood on the touchline and called out encouragement to his team, one of his assistants walked over. 'They're terrified of Erling,' he said, covering his mouth from the cameras. 'Just watch. They're pointing and scrambling every time he makes a run.'

Edin focused on the Leipzig defence and saw that his assistant was right. As Dortmund prepared to take a goal kick, Marco was within shouting distance. Edin called to him, first pointing to his eye and then making a sweeping motion with his hand.

Marco nodded. He understood: look for the ball in behind. He relayed the signs to Erling, who winked back.

Moments later, Marco found space in the centre of midfield. With a quick glance to see where Erling was, he pinged a pass behind the defence. Erling was already in a full sprint. He reached the ball first, easily won the shoulder-to-shoulder battle with his marker and took a touch to set up a shot. Despite stumbling a little as he got his left foot to the ball, Erling poked the ball under the goalkeeper and into the net.

Goooooooooooaaaaaaaaaaalllllllllllllllllllllllll!!!!!!!!!!

He ran to Marco to celebrate, and both of them pointed over to Edin, who grinned back and pumped his fist. Dortmund were in control.

In the second half, it just felt like a matter of time before Dortmund scored again on the counter-attack. As Leipzig pushed forward desperately, they left acres of grass for Jadon and Erling – and the deadly Dortmund duo made them pay. Jadon burst free, drew a defender towards him and set up Erling.

Goooooooooooooooooooooaaaaaaaaaaaaaaaaaalllllllllllllll lllllllllllll!!!!!!!!!!!!!!!!!!!!!!

Game over! Two goals for Jadon and two for Erling. There was still time left in the game, but the celebrations had already started on the Dortmund bench as the substitutes danced around. When the referee blew the full-time whistle, Erling raised his arms in the air. Everything after that was a blur – hugging his teammates, going over to the fans, celebrating with the trophy.

Back in the dressing room, he turned on his phone and stepped into one of the side rooms to video call his parents.

'What a game!' Gry Marita said, answering the call on the first ring. 'We feel like we kicked every ball with you. Congratulations, son.'

Erling smiled. 'Yeah, it'll take something pretty special to top that,' he said. 'It felt so good to score in a final, especially the second goal. Sure, it's not the Bundesliga title or the Champions League trophy, but I'm coming for those next.'

Alfie and Gry Marita grinned proudly as Erling waved and rushed off to join his teammates.

This is just the beginning, Erling thought, as he sat down with the trophy and asked one of the team physios to snap some photos of him with it.

CHAPTER 24

LIVING IN
THE MOMENT

Erling opened another pack of burgers, placed
them carefully on the barbecue and closed the lid.
He turned and looked around the garden. He had
arranged this barbecue for the Dortmund youngsters
– his teammates and friends – to give them a chance
to take a few hours away from the daily grind of
training and games. Today, there were no points to
fight for and no coaches to impress. They could just be
themselves.

He pulled up a chair and joined the circle next to
Jadon and Jude. Gio sat opposite, next to Youssoufa
Moukoko, the latest youngster catching the eye at
Dortmund.

'Some days, this all still feels like a dream,' Jude said, fiddling with his sunglasses and picking up his drink.

Erling nodded. 'I know. That's part of the reason I wanted to get us all together today. We're all on this amazing journey and things are moving so fast. None of us know how long we'll all be teammates, so we've got to make the most of every moment.' Erling had tried to ignore the rumours, but he knew there was talk of Europe's biggest clubs planning huge bids for the Dortmund core.

'Come on, man, you're going to make me cry!' Jadon joked.

Erling pretended to lean over and push him off his chair. 'You know I'm right.'

'Just having each other to talk to is pretty cool,' Gio added. 'There are so few people that know what it's like to be on this whirlwind adventure. At least we all get it.'

'The more I think about it, that's what made last season so special,' Erling said, sitting forward. 'The reality of the football business is that this kind of young core doesn't stay together forever. That's all I'm saying. Whatever the future holds, I'm just thankful we're on this journey together.'

'Me too, buddy,' Jadon replied, clinking his glass against Erling's glass. 'Cheers!'

'Cheers!' they all said.

'How are those burgers doing, Erling?' Youssoufa said suddenly.

Erling's face froze. 'Oh no!' He jumped up and rushed over to the barbecue. 'Phew, just in time!'

It had been a roller-coaster ride so far and, as Erling relaxed with teammates who had become friends, he knew there were plenty of chapters for all of them still to write. For now, all they needed was a few laughs, a little sunshine and a plate of burgers.

Read on for a sneak preview of
another brilliant football story by
Matt and Tom Oldfield. . .

MBAPPE

Available now!

CHAPTER 1

FROM RUSSIA
WITH LOVE

On 14 July 2018, Kylian sent a message to his millions of social media followers, from Russia with love: 'Happy French national day everyone. Let's hope the party continues until tomorrow night!'

'Tomorrow night' – 15 July – the French national team would be playing in the World Cup final at the Luzhniki Stadium in Moscow. It was the most important football match on the planet and Kylian's country was counting on him.

So far, he hadn't let them down at all. In fact, Kylian had been France's speedy superstar, scoring the winning goal against Denmark, and then two more in an amazing man-of-the-match performance against Argentina. That all made him the nation's best 'Number 10' since Zinedine Zidane back in 1998.

That was the year that France last won the World Cup.

That was also the year that Kylian was born.

Thanks to their new young superstar, *'Les Bleus'* were now the favourites to lift the famous golden trophy again. They had already beaten Lionel Messi's Argentina, Luis Suárez's Uruguay in the quarter-finals, and Eden Hazard's Belgium in the semi-finals. Now, the only nation standing in their way was Luka Modrić's Croatia.

'You've done so well to get this far,' the France manager, Didier Deschamps, told them as kick-off approached and the nerves began to jangle. 'Now, you just need to go out there and finish off the job!'

A massive 'Yeah!' echoed around the room. It was one big team effort, from captain Hugo Lloris in goal through to Kylian, Antoine Griezmann and Olivier Giroud in attack. Everyone worked hard and everyone worked together.

By the way, those jangling nerves didn't

belong to Kylian. No way, he was the coolest character around! He never let anything faze him. When he was younger, he hadn't just hoped to play in a World Cup final; he had expected it. It was all part of his killer plan to conquer the football world.

Out on the pitch for the final in Moscow, Kylian sang the words of the French national anthem with a big smile on his face. As a four-year-old, some people had laughed at his ambitious dreams. Well, they definitely weren't laughing now.

'Right, let's do this!' Paul Pogba clapped and cheered as they took up their positions. His partnership with Kylian would be key for France. Whenever Paul got the ball in midfield, he would look to find his pacy teammate with a perfect pass.

Kylian's first action of the final, however, was in defence. He rushed back quickly to block a Croatia cross.

'Well done!' France's centre-back Samuel Umtiti shouted.

Once that was done, it was all about attacking.

Even in a World Cup final, Kylian wasn't afraid to try his tricks and flicks. They didn't always work but it was worth the risk.

It was an end-to-end first half, full of exciting action. First, Antoine curled in a dangerous free kick and Mario Mandžukić headed the ball into his own net. 1–0 to France! Kylian punched the air – what a start!

Ivan Perišić equalised for Croatia but then he handballed it in his own box. Penalty! Antoine stepped up... and scored – 2–1 to France!

The players were happy to hear the half-time whistle blow. They needed a break to breathe and regroup. Although France were winning, they still had work to do if they wanted to become World Champions again.

'We need to calm things down and take control of the game,' Deschamps told his players. 'Stay smart out there!'

Kylian listened carefully to his manager's message. He needed to relax and play to his strengths – his skill but also his speed. This was his chance to go down in

World Cup history:

Pelé in 1958,

Diego Maradona in 1986,

Zidane in 1998,

Ronaldo in 2002,

Kylian in 2018?

In the second half, France's superstars shone much more brightly. Kylian collected Paul's long pass and sprinted straight past the Croatia centre-back. Was he about to score in his first World Cup final? No, the keeper came out to make a good save.

'Ohhhh!' the supporters groaned in disappointment.

But a few minutes later, Paul and Kylian linked up again. From wide on the right wing, Kylian dribbled towards goal. Uh-oh, the Croatia left-back was in big trouble.

With a stepover and a little hop, Kylian cut inside towards goal but in a flash, he fooled the defender with another quick change of direction.

'Go on!' the France fans urged their exciting young hero.

What next? Kylian still had two defenders in front

of him, so he pulled it back to Antoine instead. He couldn't find a way through either so he passed it on to Paul. Paul's first shot was blocked but his second flew into the bottom corner. 3–1!

Kylian threw his arms up in the air and then ran over to congratulate his friend. Surely, France had one hand on the World Cup trophy now.

Antoine had scored, and so had Paul. That meant it must be Kylian's turn next! He would have to score soon, however, in case Deschamps decided to take him off early…

When he received the pass from Lucas Hernández, Kylian was in the middle of the pitch, at least ten yards outside the penalty area. Was he too far out to shoot? No, there was no such thing as 'too far' for Kylian! He shifted the ball to the right and then BANG! He tucked the ball into the bottom corner before the keeper could even dive. 4–1!

Goooooooooooooooooooooaaaaaaaaaaaaaaaaalllllllllllllll llllllllllllll!!!!!!!!!!!!!!!!!!!!!!

As his teammates rushed over to him, Kylian had just enough time for his trademark celebration. With a

little jump, he planted his feet, folded his arms across
his chest, and tried to look as cool as he could. That
last part was really hard because he had just scored in
a World Cup final!

The next thirty minutes ticked by very slowly but
eventually, the game was over. France 4 Croatia 2 –
they were the 2018 World Champions!

Allez Les Bleus! Allez Les Bleus! Allez Les Bleus!

Kylian used the last of his energy to race around
the pitch, handing out hugs to everyone he saw: his
sad opponents, his happy teammates, his manager,
EVERYONE! In that amazing moment, he would have
hugged every single French person in the world if he
could. Instead, he blew kisses at the cameras. From
Russia with love!

And Kylian's incredible night wasn't over yet.
Wearing his country's flag around his waist, he walked
up on stage to collect the tournament's Best Young
Player award from Emmanuel Macron.

'Thank you, you're a national hero now!' the
French President told him proudly.

'My pleasure, Sir!' Kylian replied.

Would his smile ever fade? Certainly not while he had a World Cup winners' medal around his neck and the beautiful World Cup trophy in his hands. He didn't ever want to let go. Kylian kissed it and raised it high into the Moscow night sky.

'Hurray!' the fans cheered for him.

At the age of nineteen, Kylian was already living out his wildest dreams. The boy from Bondy had become a World Cup winner and football's next great superstar.

CHAPTER 2

A SPORTY FAMILY IN A SPORTY SUBURB

'What if he doesn't like sports?' Wilfried Mbappé whispered to his wife, Fayza Lamari, as they watched their new-born son, Kylian, sleeping peacefully in his cot. He was a man who loved to laugh but at that moment, he had a worried look on his face.

Fayza smiled and spoke softly so as not to wake the baby. 'Does it really matter? Kylian can do whatever he wants to do, and we're going to love him no matter what!'

Her husband nodded but she could still see the frown lines on his forehead.

'Relax, Wilfried, he's our son, so of course he's going to LOVE sports!'

With parents like his, Kylian was always destined to be a sporting superstar.

Wilfried's favourite sport was football. When he was younger, he had moved to France from Cameroon in order to find a good job. As well as that, Wilfried had also been lucky enough to find the two loves of his life – his wife, Fayza, and his local football club, AS Bondy. His playing days were now over, but he had become a youth team coach instead.

Fayza's favourite sport was handball. She was a star player for AS Bondy in France's top division. Ever since she was a kid, Fayza had been racing up and down the right wing, competing fiercely with her rivals. She couldn't wait to get back out on the court, now that Kylian was born.

'No-one messes with your mum!' Wilfried always told his sons proudly.

Not only were the Mbappés a very sporty family, but they also lived in a very sporty suburb of Paris. Over the years, so many successful athletes, basketball players and footballers had grown up in Bondy. There was top talent on display wherever you turned!

The sports club, AS Bondy, was at the heart of the local community, right in the middle of all the shops and tower blocks. Growing up, Kylian could see the local stadium from the windows of their apartment. It was an inspiring sight.

AS Bondy was a place where people from lots of different French-speaking backgrounds – Algeria, Morocco, Tunisia, Haiti, Togo, Mali, Senegal, Ivory Coast – could come together and enjoy themselves. That was really important because life wasn't easy for the local people. They had to work long hours in order to feed their families and strive towards a brighter future.

For the young people of Bondy, the sports club was particularly special. It was their home away from home, where they could develop their skills, while at the same time staying out of trouble. Coaches like Wilfried taught them three simple rules to live by:

1) Respect each other.

2) Stay humble.

3) Love sport.

At AS Bondy, youngsters could forget about their

problems and just focus on their sporting dreams.

In years to come, the local kids would look up at a big mural showing Kylian's face under the words, 'Bondy: Ville Des Possibles'. No, it wasn't the wealthiest part of Paris, but it was a 'City of Possibilities' where, with hard work and dedication, you could achieve your dreams.

So, what was Kylian's sporting dream? To play handball like his mother, or football like his father? His adopted older brother, Jirés Kembo Ekoko, was already the star of Wilfried's Under-10s football team. Would Kylian follow in his footsteps?

Or perhaps Kylian would choose to play a different sport...

'He can do whatever he wants to do,' Fayza reminded Wilfried, 'and we're going to love him no matter what!'

Growing up, Kylian enjoyed playing tennis and basketball with his friends, but there was really only one sport for him. To his dad's delight, that sport turned out to be football!

HAALAND HONOURS

Red Bull Salzburg
🏆 Austrian Bundesliga: 2018–19, 2019–20
🏆 Austrian Cup: 2018–19

Borussia Dortmund
🏆 DFB-Pokal: 2020–21

Individual
🏆 Austrian Footballer of the Year: 2019
🏆 FIFA U-20 World Cup Golden Boot: 2019
🏆 Golden Boy (Best Young Footballer in Europe): 2020

🏆 Norwegian Footballer of the Year: 2020

🏆 Bundesliga Player of the Season: 2020–21

🏆 UEFA Champions League Top Goalscorer: 2020–21

HAALAND

9

THE FACTS

NAME:
Erling Braut Haaland

DATE OF BIRTH:
21 July 2000

AGE: 20

PLACE OF BIRTH:
Leeds, England

NATIONALITY: Norway

BEST FRIENDS: Jadon Sancho
and Giovanni Reyna

CURRENT CLUB: Borussia Dortmund

POSITION: ST

THE STATS

Height (cm):	194
Club appearances:	170
Club goals:	126
Club trophies:	3
International appearances:	12
International goals:	7
International trophies:	0
Ballon d'Ors:	0

★ ★ ★ **HERO RATING: 89** ★ ★ ★

GREATEST MOMENTS

1 JULY 2018,
BRANN 0–4 MOLDE

Aged seventeen, this was the match where Erling
showed just what an unstoppable striker he could be.
The poor Brann defenders had no chance as Erling
completed his hat-trick in only fifteen minutes and
then added another six minutes later. Yes, he certainly
was a superstar in the making.

30 MAY 2019,
NORWAY 12–0 HONDURAS

After two disappointing performances at the Under-20 World Cup, Erling really came to life in this third group game, firing in a record-breaking NINE goals in ninety minutes! Even though Norway were knocked out, it was enough to win Erling the tournament's Top Scorer award and get even more people talking about his talent.

17 SEPTEMBER 2019,
RED BULL SALZBURG 6–2 GENK

In this match, his Champions League debut, Erling proved he was a big game player by destroying the Belgian club Genk with a phenomenal first-half hat-trick. By the time he walked off the pitch with the match ball tucked under his arm, all of Europe's top clubs wanted to sign him.

17 FEBRUARY 2021,
SEVILLA 2–3 BORUSSIA DORTMUND

The night after Kylian Mbappé's masterclass against Barcelona, football's other new superstar put on a big performance too. First, Erling set up Dortmund's equaliser and then he scored two of his own, plus two more in the second leg to send his team through to the Champions League quarter-finals.

13 MAY 2021,
RB LEIPZIG 1–4 BORUSSIA DORTMUND

Erling ended his sensational season on a high with two goals and the winner's trophy in this DFB-Pokal final. Even Dayot Upamecano, one of the best young defenders in the world, couldn't stop Erling from stealing the show alongside his strike partner, Jadon Sancho.

PLAY LIKE YOUR HEROES

HOW TO SCORE LIKE ERLING
'THE TERMINATOR' HAALAND

STEP 1: Although you're a striker, you're also the first defender. Put pressure on your opponents and fight hard to win the ball back. Then, once one of your teammates has possession...

STEP 2: ...*ZOOM!* Sprint forward as fast as you can, pumping your arms like it's the most important race you've ever run.

STEP 3: As you burst towards the box, look up to see where the defenders are, and adjust your movement to make sure you find the gaps.

STEP 4: 'PASS IT NOW!' Call for the ball as loudly and confidently as possible. You're the striker; it's your job to shoot and score.

STEP 5: You're into the penalty area now, with the goal in sight, but there's no need to panic. Slow down, stay calm, and take your time before...

STEP 6: *BANG!* Everyone knows about your lethal left foot, but always ask yourself, 'What's the best way to score in this situation?' A cheeky chip, a powerful smash, or a dribble around the keeper?

STEP 7: ...*GOAL!* Jump up high and punch the air, then celebrate with your friends because football is a team game.

TEST YOUR KNOWLEDGE

QUESTIONS

1. Which Premier League football club did Erling's dad play for when Erling was very young?

2. Erling broke the Under-6 world record in which Olympic event?

3. As a youngster, which two football superstars' skills did Erling want to combine?

4. How old was Erling when he made his first-team debut for Bryne?

5. What's the name of the music band that Erling formed with his friends?

6. Which legendary Norway striker did Erling work with when he moved to Molde?

7. How many goals did Erling score for Norway at the 2019 Under-20 World Cup?

8. How many goals did Erling score on his debut for Borussia Dortmund?

9. Erling is so dedicated that he sleeps next to a football – true or false?

10. How many Champions League games did it take Erling to reach twenty goals?

11. Erling scored two goals for Dortmund in the 2021 DFB-Pokal final, and who scored the other two?

10. *Fourteen – he's the fastest ever!* 11. *Jadon Sancho.*
8. *Three – yet another hat-trick!* 9. *True! Well, once anyway...*
6. *Ole Gunnar Solskjær.* 7. *Nine, all in one amazing match!*
3. *Cristiano Ronaldo and Zlatan Ibrahimović.* 4. *Fifteen!* 5. *Flow Kingz.*
1. *Manchester City.* 2. *Long Jump!*

CAN'T GET ENOUGH OF
ULTIMATE FOOTBALL HEROES?

**Check out heroesfootball.com
for quizzes, games, and competitions!**

**Plus join the Ultimate Football Heroes
Fan Club to score exclusive content
and be the first to hear about new
books and events.
heroesfootball.com/subscribe/**